Embracing the Joy Within
Unravelling the Secrets for Living a Good Life

Rebecca A. Reyes

Table of contents

Introduction

Welcome and Book Overview

Welcome to "Embracing the Joy Within: Unravelling the Secrets for Living a Good Life" – a transformative journey towards discovering the key to lasting happiness and fulfilment. In this book, we will embark on a quest to uncover the secrets that can lead us to embrace joy from within, empowering us to live a truly good life.

In today's fast-paced world, the pursuit of happiness has become a common goal for many individuals. However, happiness can often feel elusive, as we search for it in external achievements, possessions, or the approval of others. This book challenges the conventional notion of happiness and invites you to explore a deeper, more profound sense of contentment that resides within you.

The journey we are about to embark on is not a quick fix or a one-size-fits-all solution. It is a process of self-discovery and personal growth that requires patience, introspection, and a willingness to embrace change. Through the pages of this book, we will delve into various aspects of life, touching on the realms of psychology, philosophy, and practical wisdom to create a holistic approach to living a good life.

Overview of the Book:

Chapter 1: Understanding the Quest for Happiness
This chapter lays the foundation for our exploration of happiness. It delves into the universal desire for happiness and examines the different ways people seek it. By understanding the distinction between

fleeting pleasures and lasting joy, it will set the stage for a more meaningful pursuit of fulfilment.

Chapter 2: Cultivating a Positive Mindset
Our mindset plays a crucial role in shaping our experiences and perceptions. In this chapter, the power of cultivating a positive mindset and identifying the challenges of negative thought, learning to practise gratitude and appreciation, and fostering a growth mindset that empowers us to embrace challenges and opportunities.

Chapter 3: Building Meaningful Relationships
Human connections are at the core of our well-being, emphasise the importance of building and nurturing meaningful relationships. The impact of social connections on our happiness and delve into effective communication and emotional intelligence as essential tools for fostering authentic connections.

Chapter 4: Finding Fulfilment through Passion and Purpose
At the heart of living a good life lies the pursuit of passion and purpose. In the journey to identify and embrace our passions and interests, by aligning our life choices with our core values and sense of purpose, we can experience a deep sense of fulfilment.

Chapter 5: Embracing Mindfulness and Self-Compassion
Mindfulness and self-compassion are potent practices that anchor us in the present moment and cultivate kindness towards ourselves. The concept of mindfulness, learn various mindfulness techniques, and discover the transformative power of self-compassion in nurturing a healthy relationship with ourselves.

Chapter 6: Balancing Work, Life, and Leisure

Finding a harmonious balance between work, life, and leisure is essential for overall well-being. The strategies for achieving work-life balance, the importance of incorporating leisure and hobbies into our daily routines, and the significance of downtime and relaxation for sustained happiness.

Chapter 7: Grappling with Adversity and Resilience

Life is a series of challenges and obstacles, but our ability to navigate adversity with resilience defines our growth with coping mechanisms for dealing with life's setbacks, building resilience to bounce back stronger, and transforming adversity into opportunities for personal development.

Chapter 8: Embracing Change and Letting Go

Change is an inevitable part of life, and our ability to adapt determines our emotional well-being. By learning to embrace changes with openness and acceptance, we can navigate transitions and uncertainties with grace.

Chapter 9: Living a Healthy and Balanced Lifestyle
A healthy body and mind are vital for living a good life. The connection between physical health and emotional well-being, will explore the significance of incorporating exercise, nutrition, and rest into our daily routines, promoting a holistic approach to a healthy lifestyle.

Chapter 10: Spreading Joy and Kindness to Others
Acts of kindness and giving back have the power to create a positive ripple effect in the world. By cultivating empathy and compassion, we can make a meaningful impact on the lives of others and create a more harmonious society.

Conclusion:

In the concluding chapter, we will reflect on the profound journey we have taken together in search of the secrets to living a good life. We will reiterate the value of embracing joy from within and highlight the actionable steps we can take to continue our pursuit of fulfilment beyond the pages of this book.

As we embark on this transformative journey, be prepared to delve deep into the core of your being, for the secrets to living a good life lie within you. Let us begin this adventure of self-discovery, where joy, purpose, and fulfilment await us.

The Significance of Finding Joy Within

In today's fast-paced and often chaotic world, the pursuit of happiness has become a prevalent goal for many individuals. However, all too often, we seek external factors and material possessions to fill the void within us, believing that they hold the key to our happiness. What we fail to realise is that genuine and lasting joy springs from within us, waiting to be discovered and embraced.

1. The Illusion of External Fulfilment:

In our consumer-driven society, we are bombarded with messages that suggest our happiness is linked to the acquisition of possessions, status, and wealth. This external pursuit can create a never-ending cycle of desire, where satisfaction is fleeting, and the quest for happiness becomes an elusive dream. It is crucial to recognize the illusion of external fulfilment and acknowledge that true happiness does not rely on the material possessions we accumulate but rather on our internal state of being.

2. The Power of Inner Contentment:

Finding joy within ourselves grants us the power of inner contentment. Contentment is not the absence of desires but rather a state of appreciation for what we have and who we are. When we focus on cultivating inner contentment, we develop a deeper sense of gratitude and serenity that sustains us even in the face of life's challenges.

3. Nurturing Emotional Well-being:

Our emotional well-being plays a significant role in our overall happiness. By tapping into our inner joy, we can better understand and regulate our emotions, leading to improved mental health and resilience. Embracing joy within can act as a buffer against stress, anxiety, and depression, providing us with a stable emotional foundation to navigate life's ups and downs.

4. The Fulfilment of Self-Discovery:

Discovering joy within ourselves involves a journey of self-discovery. Through introspection and self-awareness, we uncover our passions, values, and authentic selves. This process allows us to align our actions with our true desires and purpose, leading to a profound sense of fulfilment and purpose in life.

5. Breaking Free from External Validation:

Relying on external sources for validation can be a never-ending cycle of seeking approval from others. Embracing joy within means acknowledging our inherent worth and finding validation from ourselves rather than seeking it from external sources. This liberation empowers us to make choices based on our genuine desires and beliefs, leading to a more fulfilling and authentic life.

6. Embracing Imperfections and Self-compassion:

Finding joy within ourselves requires us to embrace our imperfections and practice self-compassion. We are all human and bound to make mistakes, but learning to be kind to ourselves in these moments of vulnerability is crucial to our well-being. Embracing self-compassion allows us to grow and evolve without being burdened by self-criticism, leading to greater inner peace and happiness.

7. Building Resilience and Coping with Challenges:

Life is filled with challenges and uncertainties. Embracing joy within equips us with resilience, the ability to bounce back from setbacks, and the courage to face adversity with a positive mindset. Resilience enables us to view challenges as opportunities for growth and transformation, fostering a sense of strength and optimism in the face of difficulties.

Finding joy within ourselves is a transformative journey that leads to a deeper understanding of our true selves and our place in the world. By recognizing the significance of inner joy and its impact on our emotional well-being, self-fulfilment, and resilience, we open the door to a more meaningful and joyful life. In the following chapters, we will explore practical strategies and insights to help you cultivate this inner joy and unravel the secrets for living a good life. Let us embark on this enlightening expedition together, as we discover the power of embracing the joy within.

Setting the Stage for a Fulfilling Life

In the quest for a fulfilling life, one must first set the stage for the journey ahead. The foundation upon which we build our lives plays a crucial role in determining our overall happiness and sense of contentment. In this section, we will delve into the essential elements that lay the groundwork for a life filled with purpose, joy, and fulfilment.

The concept of a fulfilling life goes beyond mere material possessions and achievements. It encompasses a deeper understanding of oneself, the pursuit of meaningful relationships, and the alignment of our actions with our core values and aspirations. Let us embark on this exploration of the essential components that will shape our path to a life worth living.

1. Self-Reflection and Self-Discovery:
   Before we can navigate the path to fulfilment, we must embark on a journey of self-reflection and self-discovery. Understanding our true selves, our passions, strengths, and weaknesses, will help us chart a course that resonates with our authentic selves. Take the time to introspect

and ask yourself meaningful questions:
What brings you joy? What are your deepest
aspirations? What values do you hold dear?
This process of introspection will be the
guiding light in shaping your vision of a
fulfilling life.

2. Defining Personal Goals and Aspirations:
   Once we have gained insight into our inner
world, it is time to set meaningful and
achievable goals. Your goals should align
with your values, passions, and sense of
purpose. Whether they are related to career,
personal growth, relationships, or
experiences, well-defined goals serve as
stepping stones towards fulfilment. As you
set your sights on these objectives,
remember to keep them realistic and
flexible, allowing room for growth and
adaptation along the way.

3. Cultivating a Positive Mindset:
   The power of a positive mindset cannot be
overstated. Our thoughts and beliefs shape

our reality, influencing our emotions, actions, and overall well-being. Embrace optimism and cultivate a mindset that focuses on solutions rather than dwelling on problems. Challenges are part of life's journey, but with a positive perspective, they become opportunities for growth and learning.

4. Embracing Change and Adaptability:
  Change is an inevitable part of life, and learning to embrace it with an open mind is crucial for a fulfilling existence. Often, the fear of change can hinder our progress and prevent us from stepping outside our comfort zones. Embrace change as a means of growth and expansion, and be open to new experiences that may lead to unexpected joys and revelations.

5. Gratitude and Appreciation:
  Expressing gratitude for the blessings in our lives can transform our perspective and enhance our overall well-being. By

acknowledging and appreciating the little joys, the supportive relationships, and the opportunities that come our way, we cultivate a sense of abundance and contentment. Gratitude allows us to find joy in the present moment and fosters a positive outlook on life.

6. Nurturing Supportive Relationships:
   Meaningful and supportive relationships play a pivotal role in our pursuit of fulfilment. Surround yourself with individuals who uplift and inspire you. Cultivate deep connections based on trust, empathy, and mutual understanding. As social beings, our interactions with others contribute significantly to our emotional well-being and overall satisfaction with life.

7. Embracing a Growth Mindset:
   A growth mindset propels us towards continuous learning and self-improvement. Embrace challenges and view failures as opportunities to learn and evolve. Embrace

a mindset that sees potential for growth in every aspect of life, encouraging personal development and paving the way for a more fulfilling journey.

Setting the stage for a fulfilling life requires a combination of introspection, goal-setting, positive mindset, and embracing change. The journey ahead may not always be smooth, but armed with these foundational elements, you are well-prepared to navigate the twists and turns that life presents. Let us now move forward with a sense of purpose, determined to uncover the secrets of living a good life filled with joy and contentment.

Chapter 1:Understanding the Quest for Happiness

The Pursuit of Happiness - A Universal Desire

Happiness, the elusive yet universal quest of humanity, has captivated the hearts and minds of individuals throughout history. From ancient philosophers to modern scholars, the concept of happiness has been explored, contemplated, and sought after by people from all walks of life. It is a feeling we all yearn for, an emotion that transcends cultural boundaries and societal norms. In this section, we delve into the profound desire for happiness and why it remains an intrinsic part of the human experience.

At its core, the pursuit of happiness is a fundamental aspect of human nature. As sentient beings, we are naturally inclined to seek pleasure and avoid pain. Happiness, in its essence, represents the ultimate form of pleasure and fulfilment, making it a goal that resonates with every individual. It is an aspiration that transcends age, gender, ethnicity, and socioeconomic status. From the innocent laughter of a child to the wisdom of a seasoned elder, the yearning for happiness is a shared sentiment that binds humanity together.

Throughout history, various civilizations and belief systems have contemplated the nature of happiness and its role in the human experience. Ancient Greek philosophers, such as Aristotle, believed that happiness, or eudaimonia, is the ultimate goal of human life. They argued that true happiness lies in living a life of virtue and excellence, finding purpose and fulfilment in virtuous actions and meaningful pursuits.

In more recent times, psychologists and researchers have dedicated significant efforts to understanding happiness from a scientific perspective. The field of positive psychology emerged, focusing on the study of human well-being and flourishing. Scholars like Martin Seligman and Mihaly Csikszentmihalyi have explored the concept of "flow," a state of deep engagement and contentment that arises when individuals are fully absorbed in an enjoyable and challenging activity.

While the quest for happiness is universal, its pursuit can take on different forms and expressions across cultures. Cultural values, norms, and expectations can shape how individuals perceive and seek happiness. For some, happiness may be closely tied to material wealth and success, while for others, it may be rooted in spiritual growth and connection. Understanding these cultural variations can provide valuable insights into the diverse ways people approach happiness and well-being.

The pursuit of happiness is not solely driven by individual desires. Societies, too, have recognized the importance of promoting happiness and well-being for their citizens. Countries like Bhutan have adopted a unique measure of progress called Gross National Happiness (GNH), which takes into account not just economic indicators but also social, environmental, and psychological well-being.

In the fast-paced and consumer-driven world we live in today, the quest for happiness can sometimes be overshadowed by external pressures and societal expectations. The constant pursuit of material possessions and societal approval may lead individuals away from genuine sources of joy and fulfilment. This raises the question of whether happiness lies in external achievements or whether it is an internal state that can be cultivated regardless of external circumstances.

In conclusion, the pursuit of happiness is an intrinsic part of the human experience, transcending time, culture, and geographical boundaries. It is a universal desire that connects us all, driving us to seek fulfilment, joy, and contentment in our lives. From ancient philosophical teachings to modern scientific research, understanding happiness has been a subject of profound exploration. As we embark on this journey of uncovering the secrets to living a good life and embracing the joy within, let us recognize that happiness is not just a destination but a lifelong journey of self-discovery and growth. It is a journey that invites us to explore the depths of our souls, cultivate positive mindsets, and nurture meaningful connections with others. In the subsequent chapters, we will delve deeper into the various aspects of happiness, offering practical insights and actionable strategies for embracing joy within and leading a good life.

Differentiating between Fleeting Pleasure and Lasting Joy

In the pursuit of happiness, it's essential to recognize the difference between fleeting pleasure and lasting joy. While pleasure and joy might seem synonymous at first glance, they stem from distinct sources and have divergent effects on our well-being. Understanding this distinction is crucial in our quest for a fulfilling life, as it allows us to make conscious choices that promote genuine and lasting happiness.

The Nature of Fleeting Pleasure

Fleeting pleasure is often associated with short-lived, surface-level experiences that provide temporary satisfaction. These moments of pleasure might arise from indulging in our favourite dessert, going on a shopping spree, or spending a weekend at an amusement park. While these experiences can be enjoyable and bring momentary happiness, they are often external and dependent on external circumstances.

The allure of fleeting pleasure lies in its immediate gratification. It offers a quick escape from stress or boredom, providing a burst of positive emotions. However, this pleasure is transient and can leave us craving more, leading to a cycle of seeking instant gratification without addressing deeper aspects of well-being.

The Essence of Lasting Joy

In contrast, lasting joy is an internal state of contentment and fulfilment that transcends momentary pleasures. It emanates from a deeper sense of purpose, meaningful connections, and personal growth. Lasting joy is not solely reliant on external factors but is cultivated through our mindset and the choices we make in life.

Lasting joy emerges when we align our actions with our core values and engage in activities that bring a sense of purpose and fulfilment. It can be found in pursuing meaningful goals, practising gratitude, and nurturing genuine relationships. Unlike fleeting pleasure, lasting joy provides a stable foundation for our well-being, allowing us to navigate life's challenges with resilience and optimism.

Cultivating Lasting Joy

Cultivating lasting joy requires introspection and a willingness to explore our inner landscape. Here are some essential steps to foster lasting joy in our lives:

1. Reflect on Values and Priorities: Take time to identify your core values and what truly matters to you. Consider what brings you a sense of fulfilment and align your choices with these values.

2. Mindful Living:Embrace mindfulness practices that encourage living in the present moment. Mindfulness helps us savour positive experiences, appreciate simple pleasures, and develop a deeper connection with ourselves and others.

3. Gratitude Practice:Develop a habit of expressing gratitude daily. Acknowledge and appreciate the blessings, big and small, in your life. Gratitude shifts our focus from what we lack to what we have, fostering a sense of abundance and contentment.

4. Seek Meaningful Connections:Nurture authentic relationships with family, friends, and community. Meaningful connections provide support, love, and a sense of belonging, enhancing our overall well-being.

5. Embrace Growth and Learning:Engage in activities that challenge you and encourage personal growth. Lifelong learning and

embracing new experiences can lead to a sense of accomplishment and fulfilment.

6. Balance Pleasure with Purpose: While it's okay to indulge in moments of pleasure, ensure they align with your values and don't become the sole focus of your pursuit of happiness.

In understanding the distinction between fleeting pleasure and lasting joy, we gain insight into the multifaceted nature of happiness. While pleasure can add colour to our lives, lasting joy provides a foundation of contentment and purpose. By prioritising lasting joy and incorporating practices that cultivate it, we pave the way for a more fulfilling and meaningful life. The journey to true happiness begins with recognizing the power of internal joy and embracing the choices that nurture it.

Examining the Impact of Positive Emotions on Overall Well-Being

Positive emotions are not merely fleeting moments of happiness; they play a profound role in shaping our overall well-being and influencing various aspects of our lives. In this section, we will delve into the science behind positive emotions, understanding their effects on physical health, mental well-being, and social interactions. By exploring the power of positivity, we can begin to appreciate the true significance of embracing joy within and its impact on living a good life.

1. The Science of Positive Emotions
   Positive emotions encompass a wide range of feelings, such as joy, gratitude, contentment, and love. Scientific research has shown that these emotions trigger various physiological and neurological responses in our bodies. When we experience positive emotions, our brain releases neurotransmitters like dopamine and endorphins, commonly known as

"feel-good" chemicals. These chemicals create a sense of pleasure and reward, contributing to our overall happiness and well-being.

Studies have also revealed that positive emotions can counteract the effects of stress on the body. They help reduce the production of cortisol, the stress hormone, thereby lowering stress levels and promoting better physical health. This interplay between positive emotions and our biology highlights the importance of cultivating joy and happiness as part of our daily lives.

2. The Role of Positive Emotions in Mental Health
Beyond the physical benefits, positive emotions also have a profound impact on mental health. Embracing joy within and experiencing positive emotions regularly can lead to increased resilience in the face of adversity. When we cultivate positive

emotions, we develop better coping mechanisms and problem-solving skills, enabling us to navigate life's challenges with greater ease.

Positive emotions are closely linked to psychological well-being and play a significant role in reducing symptoms of anxiety and depression. Engaging in activities that evoke positive emotions, such as spending time with loved ones, pursuing hobbies, or practising mindfulness, can contribute to improved mental health and overall life satisfaction.

3. Enhancing Social Connections through Positivity
Positive emotions act as social lubricants, fostering meaningful connections with others. When we experience joy and share it with those around us, it creates a positive feedback loop, strengthening our relationships and promoting a sense of belonging. Acts of kindness and expressions

of gratitude can strengthen social bonds, leading to more fulfilling connections with friends, family, and colleagues.

Additionally, positive emotions are contagious. When we radiate positivity, it tends to uplift those in our vicinity, creating a ripple effect of happiness. By embracing joy within ourselves, we can become catalysts for positive change in our social circles and contribute to a more joyful and supportive community.

4. The Power of Positive Emotions in Achieving Goals

Positive emotions are not just pleasant experiences; they can fuel our motivation and drive to achieve our goals. When we approach tasks with a positive mindset, we are more likely to persevere and overcome obstacles. Positive emotions broaden our thinking and enhance our creativity, allowing us to explore innovative solutions to challenges.

Furthermore, positive emotions can improve our ability to learn and absorb information. When we are in a positive state of mind, our cognitive abilities are heightened, and we can absorb new knowledge more effectively. This positive outlook enhances our growth and development, paving the way for personal and professional success.

Understanding the impact of positive emotions on overall well-being is crucial for embracing joy within and leading a good life. Positive emotions go beyond momentary happiness; they have far-reaching effects on our physical health, mental well-being, social interactions, and achievement of goals. By actively cultivating positive emotions and incorporating practices that promote joy into our daily lives, we can experience a profound transformation in how we perceive the world and our place within it. In the next section, we will explore practical techniques for recognizing and embracing positive emotions to further enrich our lives and well-being.

Chapter 2: Cultivating a Positive Mindset

Recognizing and Overcoming Negative Thought Patterns

In the journey to cultivating a positive mindset, one of the most critical steps is recognizing and overcoming negative thought patterns. Our thoughts play a significant role in shaping our emotions, behaviours, and overall well-being. Unfortunately, negative thought patterns can creep into our minds and sabotage our happiness and fulfilment.

I. The Power of Thoughts
Our minds are powerful tools that shape our perceptions and interpretations of the world around us. Thoughts can be either empowering or debilitating, influencing how we feel about ourselves and others. Negative thoughts can lead to self-doubt, fear,

anxiety, and even depression. Recognizing the power of our thoughts is the first step in taking control of our mindset and steering it towards a more positive direction.

II. Identifying Negative Thought Patterns
To overcome negative thought patterns, we must first identify them. Some common negative thought patterns include:

A. Negative Self-Talk: The constant stream of self-criticism and harsh judgments we direct towards ourselves. Phrases like "I'm not good enough" or "I always mess things up" are examples of negative self-talk.

B. Catastrophizing: Magnifying the worst possible outcome of a situation and expecting the worst-case scenario to happen. This thought pattern often leads to unnecessary anxiety and stress.

C. All-or-Nothing Thinking: Seeing situations in black and white, without considering any middle ground or grey areas. This rigid thinking style can lead to unrealistic expectations and disappointment.

D. Overgeneralization: Drawing broad conclusions based on limited evidence. For instance, if one thing goes wrong, assuming that everything will go wrong.

E. Personalization: Taking things personally and attributing external events to our own shortcomings, even when they have nothing to do with us.

III. Challenging Negative Thoughts
Once we've identified these negative thought patterns, the next step is to challenge them. It's essential to recognize that our thoughts are not necessarily facts; they are interpretations of events and experiences. By challenging negative thoughts, we can create space for more positive and realistic perspectives.

A. Questioning the Evidence: Ask yourself, "Is there concrete evidence to support this negative thought?" Often, you'll find that there isn't substantial evidence to back up the negativity.

B. Seeking Alternative Explanations: Consider alternative explanations for the situation. Is there a more balanced or positive way to interpret what happened?

C. Practising Self-Compassion: Treat yourself with the same kindness and understanding you would offer a friend. Be gentle with yourself when facing challenges and setbacks.

D. Reframing Negative Statements: Transform negative statements into positive or neutral ones. For example, "I failed at this task" could become "I learned valuable lessons from this experience."

IV. Cultivating a Positive Thought Pattern
Beyond challenging negative thoughts, we
can actively cultivate a positive thought
pattern to promote a healthier mindset.

A. Gratitude Practice: Regularly express
gratitude for the positive aspects of your life.
This can be done through journaling or
simply taking a moment each day to
acknowledge the things you are thankful for.

B. Affirmations: Use positive affirmations to
reinforce self-belief and confidence. Repeat
affirmations that resonate with you, such as
"I am capable of overcoming challenges."

C. Surrounding Yourself with Positivity:
Surround yourself with positive influences,
supportive friends, and inspirational
content that uplifts and motivates you.

D. Mindfulness Meditation: Practise
mindfulness meditation to observe your
thoughts without judgement and create

space between you and your negative
thinking patterns.

V. Embracing Progress, Not Perfection
It's essential to remember that cultivating a
positive mindset is a journey, and it's okay
to have moments of negativity. Embrace the
progress you make along the way, even if it's
not perfect. Celebrate small victories and be
patient with yourself as you navigate
through this transformative process.

By recognizing and overcoming negative
thought patterns, you lay the foundation for
a more positive and fulfilling life. Embracing
positivity and mindfulness can lead to
increased happiness, improved
relationships, and a greater sense of
well-being.

Practising Gratitude and Appreciation

Practising gratitude and appreciation is a transformative habit that can profoundly impact our mindset and overall well-being..

1. The Power of Gratitude:
Gratitude is the act of acknowledging and being thankful for the positive aspects of our lives. It goes beyond simply saying "thank you" but involves cultivating a deep sense of appreciation for the people, experiences, and blessings we have. Research has shown that gratitude can lead to numerous psychological and physical benefits. Studies have found that individuals who regularly practise gratitude experience increased levels of happiness, reduced stress, and improved relationships. It can even boost our immune system and promote better sleep.

2. Shifting Focus:
In our fast-paced and often stressful lives, it's easy to get caught up in negative thinking and dwell on what we lack.

However, by incorporating gratitude into our daily routine, it can shift our focus from what's missing to what we already have. This change in perspective allows us to recognize the abundance in our lives and leads to a more positive outlook.

3. Keeping a Gratitude Journal:
One effective way to cultivate gratitude is by keeping a gratitude journal. Set aside a few minutes each day to write down things you are thankful for. It can be as simple as a beautiful sunrise, a heartfelt conversation with a friend, or a small act of kindness. Putting these positive moments into words not only reinforces them in our minds but also serves as a reminder of the goodness around us.

4. Gratitude in Challenging Times:
Practising gratitude becomes even more significant during challenging times. When facing difficulties, it might seem counterintuitive to focus on gratitude, but it

can be a powerful coping mechanism.
Finding even the tiniest things to be grateful
for can provide a source of strength and
hope amidst adversity. It helps us reframe
our perspective and reminds us of the
resilience within us.

5. Expressing Gratitude to Others:
Another way to cultivate gratitude is by
expressing it to others. Take the time to
show appreciation for the people who
positively impact your life. Write a heartfelt
thank-you note, offer a sincere compliment,
or simply say "I appreciate you." Not only
does this strengthen our connections with
others, but it also reinforces our own sense
of gratitude.

6. Mindfulness and Gratitude:
Mindfulness practices can enhance the
experience of gratitude. This awareness
allows us to notice the small joys and
blessings that we might have otherwise
overlooked. By combining mindfulness with

gratitude, we can savour and fully appreciate each moment.

7. Gratitude as a Daily Habit:
Like any habit, cultivating gratitude requires consistent effort. Make it a daily practice to pause and reflect on the things you are grateful for. It could be part of your morning or bedtime routine, or even integrated into your daily commute. The more you consciously practise gratitude, the more natural it will become, and its positive effects will ripple through your life.

Practising gratitude and appreciation is a fundamental aspect of cultivating a positive mindset. By acknowledging and expressing gratitude regularly, it can shift our perspective, enhance our well-being, and build stronger connections with others. Incorporating this powerful practice into our lives can lead us closer to living a good life filled with joy and contentment.

Fostering a Growth Mindset for Personal Development

A growth mindset is the belief that one's abilities and intelligence can be developed through dedication, effort, and continuous learning. By fostering a growth mindset, individuals open themselves up to a world of opportunities and possibilities, enabling them to navigate life's challenges with resilience and optimism.

I. Understanding the Power of a Growth Mindset

A growth mindset is the antithesis of a fixed mindset, which assumes that intelligence and abilities are innate and unchangeable. People with a growth mindset see failures and setbacks as opportunities for growth and learning, rather than as indicators of their limitations. This perspective empowers individuals to embrace challenges, persist in the face of adversity, and believe in their potential to improve.

To foster a growth mindset, individuals must first recognize the difference between fixed and growth mindsets and become aware of their own beliefs about intelligence and abilities. Acknowledging the potential for growth and improvement sets the foundation for personal development and a happier, more fulfilling life.

II. Embracing a "Yet" Mentality
One powerful aspect of a growth mindset is the incorporation of the word "yet" into one's vocabulary. Instead of saying, "I can't do this," adopting a growth mindset involves saying, "I can't do this yet, but I can learn and improve." This simple shift in language can have a profound impact on self-perception and motivation.

Encouraging a "yet" mentality fosters a sense of possibility and progress. It reminds individuals that their current abilities are not fixed but rather fluid and capable of growth. By reframing challenges as opportunities for learning and development, individuals can approach tasks with a positive and proactive attitude.

III. Embracing Effort and Embracing Failure

In a growth mindset, effort is celebrated and embraced as a stepping stone to success. Instead of fearing failure or avoiding challenges, individuals with a growth mindset recognize that effort and perseverance are essential components of personal development. They understand that genuine growth often involves encountering obstacles, making mistakes, and learning from them.

By embracing effort and failure, individuals become more resilient and open to new experiences. They become more willing to take on challenges outside of their comfort zone, knowing that even if they don't succeed immediately, the journey itself is an opportunity for growth and improvement.

IV. Cultivating a Love for Learning
Central to fostering a growth mindset is a love for learning. Individuals with a growth mindset view learning as a lifelong pursuit, recognizing that knowledge and skills can be continually developed. They seek out new opportunities for learning, whether through formal education, self-directed study, or gaining insights from others.

To cultivate a love for learning, individuals can set aside time for personal development, engage in activities that stimulate their curiosity, and surround themselves with a supportive community that values growth and intellectual exploration.

V. Setting Goals and Embracing Progress
In a growth mindset, setting goals becomes an empowering exercise in

self-improvement. Individuals establish clear and realistic objectives while recognizing that the journey towards these goals is just as important as reaching the destination.

By celebrating progress, no matter how small, individuals reinforce their growth mindset and stay motivated to continue their personal development journey. Tracking progress, acknowledging achievements, and using setbacks as opportunities for learning all contribute to a positive and proactive mindset.

VI. Nurturing a Growth Mindset in Others
Lastly, fostering a growth mindset in others can have a ripple effect, creating a supportive and empowering environment. Whether in personal relationships, educational settings, or workplaces, individuals can inspire others to embrace growth and development by modelling a growth mindset themselves, providing

encouragement, and celebrating the efforts of those around them.

Fostering a growth mindset for personal development is an essential aspect of leading a good life. Embracing the power of a growth mindset allows individuals to unlock their full potential, embrace challenges, and continuously improve. By adopting a "yet" mentality, embracing effort and failure, cultivating a love for learning, setting goals, and nurturing a growth mindset in others, individuals can embark on a transformative journey towards a happier and more fulfilling life.

Chapter 3:Building Meaningful relationships

The Role of Social Connections in Happiness

Human beings are inherently social creatures, and the quality of our social connections plays a crucial role in shaping our happiness and overall well-being..

The Importance of Social Connections:

Social connections are the threads that weave the fabric of our lives. They encompass our relationships with family, friends, colleagues, and even casual acquaintances. These connections provide us with a sense of belonging, support, and understanding, which are fundamental to our emotional and psychological health.

Numerous studies have shown a strong correlation between social connections and happiness. People with a robust network of relationships tend to experience higher levels of life satisfaction, greater emotional resilience, and reduced stress levels. Social interactions also contribute to a sense of purpose, as they offer opportunities for shared experiences, celebrations, and mutual growth.

The Impact of Meaningful Relationships:

Not all social connections are equal when it comes to fostering happiness. Meaningful relationships, characterised by trust, reciprocity, and emotional depth, have a more profound impact on our well-being. These connections provide a safe space for us to express our true selves and be accepted unconditionally.

Meaningful relationships offer emotional support during challenging times, providing

a buffer against loneliness and isolation.
When we feel heard, understood, and valued
by our loved ones, our self-esteem and
self-worth are bolstered, contributing to a
greater sense of happiness and contentment.

Building and Nurturing Meaningful
Relationships:

While social connections are essential for
happiness, it's the quality of these
connections that truly matters. Here are
some practical strategies to build and
nurture meaningful relationships:

1. Cultivate Empathy:Empathy is the ability
to understand and share the feelings of
others genuinely. By actively listening and
putting ourselves in others' shoes, we create
a deeper emotional bond and demonstrate
that we care about their well-being.

2. Be Authentic and Vulnerable:
Authenticity fosters trust and intimacy in

relationships. It's essential to be genuine and open about our thoughts and feelings, allowing others to connect with our true selves.

3. Invest Time and Effort: Building meaningful relationships requires time and effort. Regularly reaching out to friends and family, engaging in shared activities, and celebrating milestones together help strengthen the bonds between individuals.

4. Show Gratitude: Expressing gratitude for the presence and support of our loved ones reinforces the value we place on these relationships. Simple gestures like saying "thank you" or writing heartfelt notes can go a long way in nurturing connections.

5. Resolve Conflicts Constructively: Conflicts are a natural part of any relationship, but how we handle them can determine the relationship's longevity. Emphasise open communication, active

listening, and a willingness to compromise to resolve conflicts in a healthy manner.

6. Be a Positive Influence: Positivity is contagious, and being a source of encouragement and support can significantly impact the happiness of those around us. Offer a helping hand, celebrate others' successes, and provide uplifting words whenever possible.

7. Expand Your Social Circles: Building new connections and fostering diverse relationships can enrich our lives and offer fresh perspectives. Engage in social activities, join clubs or organisations aligned with your interests, and be open to meeting new people.

8. Digital Detox: While technology can connect us virtually, it's essential to balance online interactions with face-to-face connections. Consider taking occasional

digital detoxes to focus on in-person connections and strengthen bonds.

The role of social connections in happiness cannot be understated. Meaningful relationships provide us with a support system, a sense of belonging, and a deep emotional connection, all of which contribute significantly to our overall well-being. By actively nurturing and prioritising these connections, we can experience greater happiness and a more fulfilling life.

Nurturing Authentic Friendships and Family Bonds

Building meaningful relationships is at the core of leading a good life. Our connections with friends and family play a vital role in our happiness and well-being. In this section, we will explore the importance of nurturing authentic friendships and strengthening family bonds to create a support network that fosters joy and fulfilment.

I. Understanding the Significance of Authentic Friendships
Authentic friendships go beyond casual acquaintances; they are built on trust, mutual respect, and genuine care. These friendships provide a sense of belonging and understanding, allowing us to be our true selves without fear of judgement. Research has shown that people with close, authentic friendships tend to report higher levels of happiness and life satisfaction.

A. Identifying Authentic Friends
   1. Characteristics of authentic friends: loyalty, empathy, and honesty.
   2. Recognizing the value of quality over quantity in friendships.
   3. The role of shared interests and values in fostering deeper connections.

B. Nurturing and Maintaining Authentic Friendships

1. Communication as the foundation of strong friendships.

2. Active listening and empathy in fostering understanding.

3. Balancing giving and receiving support to create a mutually beneficial relationship.

II. Strengthening Family Bonds for Lasting Happiness

Family bonds can be a source of tremendous joy and support throughout life. Cultivating strong relationships within the family unit can provide a sense of security and emotional well-being.

A. Embracing the Diversity of Family Relationships

1. Nurturing relationships with immediate family members (parents, siblings, children).

2. The importance of extended family connections and maintaining ties.

3. Embracing chosen family and the significance of close friends who feel like family.

B. Effective Communication within the Family

1. Open and honest communication as the cornerstone of strong family bonds.

2. Strategies for resolving conflicts in a healthy and constructive manner.

3. Fostering a supportive and nurturing family environment.

C. Creating Meaningful Traditions and Rituals

1. The power of family traditions in strengthening bonds and creating lasting memories.

2. Celebrating milestones and special occasions together.

3. Incorporating rituals that promote a sense of togetherness and unity.

III. Balancing Personal Boundaries in
Relationships
While nurturing friendships and family
bonds is crucial, it's also essential to
maintain healthy personal boundaries to
avoid emotional exhaustion or dependency.

A. The Importance of Self-Care in
Relationships
  1. Recognizing the need for self-care to
foster healthy relationships.
  2. Setting aside time for personal interests
and hobbies.
  3. Communicating boundaries with loved
ones to avoid burnout.

B. Dealing with Toxic Relationships
  1. Identifying signs of toxic friendships or
family dynamics.
  2. Strategies for addressing and managing
toxic relationships.
  3. Seeking support and professional
guidance if needed.

IV. Fostering Empathy and Emotional Support in Relationships

Authentic friendships and family bonds thrive on emotional support and understanding. Cultivating empathy within these relationships can create a strong sense of connection.

A. Practising Empathy and Active Listening
  1. The power of empathy in validating emotions and experiences.
  2. Active listening techniques to enhance understanding and connection.
  3. Being present and attentive in conversations to support loved ones effectively.

B. Providing Emotional Support During Difficult Times
  1. Offering a compassionate presence during challenging moments.
  2. Being a reliable source of comfort and encouragement.

3. The healing impact of sharing emotions and experiences in a safe space.

In nurturing authentic friendships and family bonds, we build a network of love, trust, and understanding that uplifts us during both joyful and challenging times. These relationships offer us a sense of belonging, strengthen our resilience, and contribute significantly to leading a good life filled with happiness and fulfilment. Remember, investing time and effort in cultivating these connections is a valuable investment in your overall well-being.

Communication and Emotional Intelligence in Relationships

In building meaningful relationships, effective communication and emotional intelligence play pivotal roles. These two interconnected aspects form the foundation for fostering strong and lasting connections with others.

I. The Power of Communication in Relationships

Effective communication is the lifeblood of any successful relationship. It is the bridge that connects individuals, allowing them to share thoughts, feelings, and experiences. Communication goes beyond mere words; it involves active listening, empathy, and understanding. When we communicate openly and honestly, we create an environment of trust and vulnerability, strengthening the bond with our loved ones.

A. Active Listening

True communication begins with active listening. Being fully present and engaged when someone is speaking demonstrates respect and validates their feelings. Active listening involves maintaining eye contact, nodding in acknowledgment, and providing verbal cues to show that we are genuinely interested in what the other person has to say. By practising active listening, we make others feel heard and valued, enhancing the quality of our relationships.

B. Empathy in Communication

Empathy is the ability to understand and share the feelings of another person. When we approach communication with empathy, we step into the shoes of our loved ones, acknowledging their emotions without judgement. Demonstrating empathy helps create an emotional connection, making it easier to navigate challenges and celebrate joys together. Empathetic communication fosters a sense of safety, allowing individuals to express themselves authentically.

C. Resolving Conflicts through Communication

Conflict is a natural part of any relationship, but how we handle it can make or break the connection. Effective communication allows us to address conflicts constructively, without resorting to hostility or defensiveness. By using "I" statements and expressing our feelings calmly, we encourage open dialogue and find mutually beneficial solutions. Healthy conflict resolution strengthens relationships and fosters growth.

II. Emotional Intelligence: The Key to Deeper Connections

Emotional intelligence (EI) is the ability to understand, manage, and express emotions effectively. In the context of relationships, EI enables us to navigate emotions skillfully, enhancing our understanding of ourselves and others.

A. Self-Awareness

Emotional intelligence begins with self-awareness - recognizing and understanding our own emotions. By being in tune with our feelings, we gain insight into our reactions and behaviours, making it easier to communicate our needs and boundaries to others. Self-awareness also prevents emotional reactions from dictating our actions, leading to more thoughtful and considerate communication.

B. Empathy and Emotional Regulation

Empathy is a cornerstone of emotional intelligence. As we develop empathy, we become more attuned to the emotions of those around us, fostering deeper connections. Moreover, emotional intelligence equips us with the ability to regulate our emotions, preventing impulsive reactions in heated situations. By staying composed and empathetic, we can approach conflicts with a level head and find common ground.

C. Recognizing and Validating Emotions

Emotional intelligence enables us to recognize and validate the emotions of others. When we acknowledge someone's feelings without judgement, we show genuine care and concern. Validating emotions doesn't mean we have to agree with everything; it means we respect the other person's perspective and emotions, fostering a sense of safety and acceptance in the relationship.

III. Integrating Communication and Emotional Intelligence

Bringing together effective communication and emotional intelligence amplifies the depth and intimacy of our relationships. When we practise empathetic communication, we nurture emotional connections and create a safe space for vulnerability.

A. Emotionally Intelligent Communication

Emotionally intelligent communication involves using our understanding of emotions to navigate conversations effectively. We consider the emotions of both ourselves and the other person, seeking common ground and compromises when needed. This approach fosters understanding, empathy, and trust, strengthening the relationship over time.

B. Expressing Gratitude and Affection

Incorporating emotional intelligence into communication extends to expressing gratitude and affection. Recognizing and appreciating the positive contributions of our loved ones strengthens the emotional bond. Simple acts like saying "thank you" or offering a heartfelt compliment can go a long way in making someone feel valued and cherished.

C. Honouring Boundaries and Practising Forgiveness

Emotional intelligence also involves respecting boundaries and practising forgiveness. By being attuned to each other's limits and needs, we cultivate an environment of respect and trust. Additionally, emotional intelligence allows us to forgive and let go of past grievances, fostering emotional growth and healing within the relationship.

Effective communication and emotional intelligence are essential components of building meaningful relationships. By practising active listening, empathy, and conflict resolution, we create an atmosphere of trust and understanding. Integrating emotional intelligence into communication enhances our connections by promoting self-awareness, empathy, and emotional regulation.

Chapter 4: Finding Fulfilment through Passion and Purpose

Identifying Personal Passions and Interests

In the pursuit of living a fulfilling life, one of the essential steps is to identify and embrace our personal passions and interests. Our passions are like the compass that guides us towards a sense of purpose and satisfaction. When we engage in activities that resonate with our true selves, we experience a profound sense of joy and fulfilment.

1. Understanding the Essence of Passions:

Passions are the things that ignite a fire within us, the activities that make us feel alive and energised. They can be hobbies, creative pursuits, causes we deeply care about, or areas where we feel a strong sense of purpose. Identifying our passions requires self-reflection and introspection to uncover what truly brings us joy. Often, our passions are the activities that we lose track of time while doing, the ones that make us feel completely immersed and fulfilled.

2. Reflecting on Past and Present Interests:

To begin the journey of identifying our passions, it is helpful to reflect on our past and present interests. We can take a trip down memory lane and recall the activities that have brought us joy throughout our lives. From childhood to adulthood, there might be recurring themes or patterns that point towards our passions. Additionally, examining our current interests and what excites us in the present moment can provide valuable clues about our true passions.

3. Exploring Curiosity and Trying New Things:

Sometimes, we might not be fully aware of our passions until we explore new things and step outside our comfort zones. Embracing curiosity and trying different activities can be a gateway to discovering hidden passions. Taking up new hobbies, attending workshops, or volunteering for a cause we care about can lead us to unexpected revelations about what truly brings fulfilment to our lives.

4. Assessing Values and Beliefs:

Our passions are often deeply connected to our core values and beliefs. Reflecting on what matters most to us can shed light on the activities and causes that align with our principles. For example, if environmental conservation is a core value, engaging in activities that promote sustainability and conservation efforts can become a source of passion and purpose.

5. Embracing Passion-Driven Goals:

Once we have identified our passions, the next step is to align our goals with our newfound sense of purpose. Setting passion-driven goals can be highly motivating and empowering. It allows us to channel our energy and efforts towards activities that truly matter to us, increasing the likelihood of success and fulfilment.

6. Overcoming Challenges and Fear:

Discovering our passions and pursuing them might not always be smooth sailing. We might encounter challenges and fears that stand in the way of fully embracing our passions. It's essential to acknowledge these obstacles and find ways to overcome them. Cultivating a growth mindset and seeking support from like-minded individuals can help us navigate the uncertainties and doubts that come with pursuing our passions.

7. Embracing a Lifelong Journey:

Identifying our passions is not a one-time event but rather a lifelong journey of self-discovery and growth. As we evolve and experience different stages of life, our passions might shift and evolve as well. Embracing this fluidity allows us to stay open to new experiences and continue seeking fulfilment throughout our lives.

Identifying personal passions and interests is a pivotal step on the path to living a purpose-driven and fulfilling life. By understanding the essence of our passions, reflecting on past and present interests, exploring curiosity, assessing values, and embracing passion-driven goals, we can unlock the key to genuine joy and contentment. Although challenges and fears may arise, approaching this journey with an open heart and a growth mindset enables us to embrace a lifelong adventure of self-discovery and fulfilment. Remember, the pursuit of our passions is not only an act of self-love but also a gift we give to the world as we share our unique gifts and talents with others.

Aligning Life Choices with Core Values and Purpose

In the journey to finding fulfilment through passion and purpose, one crucial aspect is aligning life choices with core values and purpose. This section delves into the significance of understanding personal values, defining a clear purpose, and making conscious decisions that resonate with one's authentic self. When individuals live in harmony with their values and purpose, they experience a profound sense of fulfilment, direction, and contentment in life.

Understanding Personal Values:

Values are the fundamental beliefs and principles that guide our actions, behaviours, and decisions. They act as a compass, steering us toward what we find meaningful and important. To align life choices with core values, it is essential to first identify and understand what these values are. This self-awareness process involves introspection and reflection on one's experiences, beliefs, and what truly matters.

Identifying personal values can be an enlightening exercise. Some common core values may include honesty, compassion, creativity, family, health, integrity, freedom, and growth. However, each person's set of values is unique and may evolve over time as life circumstances change.

Defining a Clear Purpose:

Once individuals have a deeper understanding of their core values, the next step is to define a clear purpose that aligns with those values. Purpose is the driving force that gives meaning to our lives and ignites our passions. It is the reason why we get up in the morning, the ultimate goal we strive to achieve, and the impact we desire to make in the world.

Discovering one's purpose requires soul-searching and asking profound questions. What brings a sense of joy and fulfilment? What problems or causes deeply resonate with us? How can we use our unique talents and strengths to contribute positively to society? Finding purpose might not happen overnight, but by exploring different interests and experiences, individuals can gradually unveil their true calling.

Making Conscious Decisions:

With a clear understanding of personal values and a defined purpose, it becomes easier to make conscious decisions aligned with these guiding principles. Every choice we make, whether big or small, has the potential to either lead us closer to our purpose or steer us away from it. Hence, it is vital to evaluate each decision against the yardstick of our values and purpose.

In various aspects of life, such as career choices, relationships, and lifestyle, individuals can apply this conscious decision-making approach. For example, when considering a career path, it is essential to assess whether the job aligns with one's values, whether it allows for the expression of purpose, and whether it brings a sense of fulfilment and passion.

Navigating Challenges and Staying True to Values and Purpose:

As individuals strive to align their life choices with core values and purpose, they may encounter challenges and temptations that could lead them astray. Peer pressure, societal expectations, and fear of change might test their commitment to living authentically.

During these challenging times, it is essential to stay grounded in self-awareness and revisit the essence of one's values and purpose. Regular reflection, meditation, or journaling can serve as powerful tools for maintaining focus and recentering on the journey toward fulfilment.

Embracing Growth and Evolution:

It is important to acknowledge that values and purpose can evolve over time. Life experiences, new insights, and personal growth may lead to shifts in what we hold dear and the direction we want to take. Embracing growth and allowing our values and purpose to adapt is a natural part of the journey.

Aligning life choices with core values and purpose is a transformative process that empowers individuals to lead a fulfilled life. Understanding personal values, defining a clear purpose, and making conscious decisions pave the way for a life lived authentically and in harmony with one's passions. Navigating challenges and embracing growth throughout this journey adds depth and richness to the pursuit of fulfilment. Remember, when you align your life with what truly matters to you, you unlock the door to a life of purpose, joy, and contentment.

Pursuing Goals that Bring a Sense of Fulfilment

In our journey toward living a good life and embracing the joy within, one crucial aspect is the pursuit of goals that align with our passions and values. Fulfilment comes from the satisfaction of achieving meaningful objectives that resonate deeply with our inner selves. In this section, we will explore the significance of setting purpose-driven goals, understanding the connection between passion and fulfilment, and practical strategies for pursuing and achieving these aspirations.

1. Understanding Purpose-Driven Goals:

To embark on a path of fulfilment, it is essential to understand the concept of purpose-driven goals. These goals are not merely dictated by societal expectations or external pressures; rather, they are anchored in our true desires and values. Purpose-driven goals are unique to each individual, reflecting their personal dreams and aspirations. When we set such goals, we become more motivated and invested in the journey, making the process of reaching them more gratifying.

2. Aligning Goals with Passions:

Passions are the driving force behind our purpose-driven goals. Identifying and aligning our goals with our passions creates a powerful synergy that propels us forward with unwavering determination. When we engage in activities that ignite our passions, we are more likely to experience flow states, where time seems to stand still, and our focus is fully immersed in the present moment. This heightened state of concentration not only enhances our performance but also deepens our sense of fulfilment.

3. Embracing the Journey, Not Just the Destination:

As we pursue our purpose-driven goals, it is crucial to cherish the journey rather than solely focusing on the end result. The process of growth, learning, and self-discovery along the way adds richness to our experiences. Celebrating small victories and acknowledging progress boosts our motivation and reinforces our commitment to the path we have chosen.

4. Overcoming Challenges and Obstacles:

The pursuit of purpose-driven goals is not without its challenges. It is essential to anticipate and prepare for obstacles that may arise on our journey. Cultivating resilience and adaptability helps us navigate through setbacks and setbacks with grace and determination. Each challenge we overcome becomes an opportunity for growth and self-improvement, reinforcing our sense of fulfilment when we ultimately achieve our goals.

5. Creating a Well-Defined Action Plan:

To turn our aspirations into reality, we need a well-defined action plan. Breaking down our purpose-driven goals into smaller, achievable steps provides clarity and direction. Each step becomes a milestone to celebrate, propelling us forward toward the bigger picture. A structured action plan also helps us stay organised and focused, preventing us from feeling overwhelmed or lost in the process.

6. Cultivating Patience and Persistence:

The pursuit of purpose-driven goals may require time and patience. It is essential to maintain a sense of perseverance and not be discouraged by temporary setbacks or delays. Rome wasn't built in a day, and neither are our most significant achievements. Cultivating patience allows us to savour the journey and remain committed to our goals, even when progress seems slow.

7. Embracing Continuous Growth and Learning:

A life of fulfilment is marked by continuous growth and learning. As we achieve our purpose-driven goals, new aspirations and dreams may emerge. Embracing a growth mindset encourages us to seek new challenges and expand our horizons. Learning from our experiences, both successes, and failures, equips us with valuable insights to apply in future endeavours.

8. Balancing Personal and Professional Goals:

While pursuing purpose-driven goals, it is essential to strike a balance between personal and professional aspirations. Both aspects of our lives contribute to our overall sense of fulfilment. Neglecting one at the expense of the other can lead to dissatisfaction and inner conflict. Integrating personal and professional goals allows us to lead a harmonious and fulfilling life.

The pursuit of purpose-driven goals that align with our passions and values is a transformative journey. By understanding the significance of these goals, aligning them with our passions, embracing the journey, overcoming challenges, and persisting with patience, we pave the way for a life of fulfilment. The process of pursuing and achieving purpose-driven goals enriches our experiences and deepens our connection to ourselves and the world around us. Embrace the power of purpose and passion in shaping a life that brings you true fulfilment and joy within.

Chapter 5:Embracing Mindfulness and Self-Compassion

Understanding the Concept of Mindfulness and Its Benefits

Mindfulness is a powerful practice that has gained significant popularity in recent years due to its profound impact on mental well-being and overall quality of life. This section explores the concept of mindfulness, its origins, and the numerous benefits it offers to those who embrace it in their lives.

1. What is Mindfulness?

Mindfulness, in its essence, refers to the act of being fully present and aware of our thoughts, emotions, bodily sensations, and the surrounding environment without judgement. It involves paying attention to the present moment, acknowledging it as it is, and accepting it without trying to change it or get lost in past regrets or future worries. Mindfulness has its roots in ancient Eastern philosophies, particularly in Buddhist meditation practices, but its principles have been adapted and integrated into various modern therapeutic approaches.

2. The Origins of Mindfulness

The origins of mindfulness can be traced back to ancient contemplative practices in India over two millennia ago. It was an integral part of Buddhist teachings and was often used as a way to develop insight and achieve liberation from suffering. The Pali word "sati" and the Sanskrit word "smṛti" both translate to mindfulness or awareness, reflecting the importance and universality of this practice across different cultures and languages.

3. The Science Behind Mindfulness

In recent decades, mindfulness has become the subject of extensive scientific research, validating its efficacy and numerous benefits. Studies have shown that regular mindfulness practice can lead to structural changes in the brain, particularly in regions associated with emotional regulation, memory, and stress response. This neuroplasticity highlights the brain's ability to adapt and change in response to mindfulness practice, enhancing mental resilience and emotional well-being.

4. The Benefits of Mindfulness

a. Reduced Stress and Anxiety: Mindfulness has been found to be a powerful tool in managing stress and anxiety. By fostering present-moment awareness and non-judgmental acceptance, individuals can break free from the cycle of rumination and worry, leading to reduced stress levels and enhanced emotional stability.

b. Improved Focus and Concentration: Practising mindfulness trains the mind to stay focused on the present task, reducing distractions and increasing overall attention span. This enhanced cognitive ability can lead to improved productivity and better performance in daily activities.

c. Enhanced Emotional Regulation: Mindfulness allows individuals to observe their emotions without being overwhelmed by them. This non-reactive approach enables better emotional regulation, leading to more constructive responses to challenging situations.

d. Increased Self-Awareness: Through mindfulness, individuals gain a deeper understanding of their thought patterns, beliefs, and behaviours. This heightened self-awareness can pave the way for personal growth, self-compassion, and positive changes in one's life.

e. Better Physical Health: Mindfulness has been associated with improved physical health outcomes, such as lower blood pressure, reduced inflammation, and enhanced immune function. The mind-body connection fostered by mindfulness contributes to overall well-being.

f. Enhanced Relationship Skills: By being fully present in interactions, mindful individuals can cultivate deeper connections and empathy in their relationships. Improved communication and active listening skills can lead to healthier and more meaningful connections with others.

5. Incorporating Mindfulness into Daily Life

Integrating mindfulness into daily life doesn't necessarily require long meditation sessions; it can be as simple as paying attention to the sensations while eating, taking a mindful walk, or practising deep

breathing during moments of stress.
Consistency is key, and even brief moments
of mindfulness throughout the day can
accumulate and bring about positive
changes over time.

Understanding the concept of mindfulness
is the first step toward embracing its
benefits. By being present, non-judgmental,
and aware of our experiences, we can
cultivate a more balanced and fulfilling life.
The evidence supporting the advantages of
mindfulness is compelling, and with
practice, individuals can harness its
potential to enhance their mental,
emotional, and physical well-being.
Embracing mindfulness can truly be
transformative, opening the door to a more
meaningful and joyous existence.

Practising Self-Compassion and Reducing Self-Criticism

In the journey to living a good life and embracing joy within, one of the most crucial practices is cultivating self-compassion and reducing self-criticism. Far too often, we can be our harshest critics, constantly berating ourselves for perceived flaws and mistakes. However, by learning to treat ourselves with kindness, understanding, and compassion, we can foster a more positive and nurturing relationship with ourselves.

1. Understanding Self-Compassion:

Self-compassion is the act of extending the same compassion, care, and empathy to ourselves that we would offer to a dear friend in times of struggle or difficulty. It involves recognizing our own suffering, acknowledging that it is a shared human experience, and responding with warmth and understanding. Self-compassion involves three core elements, as defined by

Dr. Kristin Neff, a leading researcher in the field:

a. Self-Kindness: Instead of being self-critical and judgmental, we learn to treat ourselves with kindness and gentleness, particularly during challenging moments.

b. Common Humanity: Recognizing that everyone experiences pain, failure, and imperfection. Understanding that we are not alone in our struggles helps foster a sense of connection and belonging.

c. Mindfulness: Being mindful involves acknowledging our feelings and thoughts without judgement. It allows us to observe our experiences with openness and curiosity.

2. The Power of Self-Compassion:

Practising self-compassion can have profound effects on our overall well-being and happiness. Numerous studies have shown that individuals who regularly engage in self-compassion experience reduced levels of stress, anxiety, and depression. They also exhibit higher levels of resilience and greater emotional stability. When we treat ourselves with kindness and understanding, we create a safe space to explore our emotions and vulnerabilities, leading to increased self-awareness and personal growth.

3. Challenging Self-Criticism:

Reducing self-criticism begins with recognizing the patterns of negative self-talk and understanding their origins. Often, these critical inner voices are shaped by societal expectations, past experiences, or comparisons with others. Identifying and challenging these destructive thought patterns is a crucial step towards fostering self-compassion.

4. Practising Self-Compassion Techniques:

a. Self-Compassionate Writing: Engage in journaling exercises where you write down self-compassionate messages to yourself. Treat yourself with the same compassion and care that you would offer a close friend facing a similar situation.

b. Loving-Kindness Meditation: Incorporate loving-kindness meditation into your daily routine. This practice involves sending love, compassion, and well-wishes to yourself and others. Repeat affirmations such as, "May I be happy, may I be healthy, may I be safe."

c. Embracing Imperfections: Embrace your imperfections and understand that they are a natural part of being human. Celebrate your uniqueness and see imperfections as opportunities for growth and learning.

d. Setting Realistic Expectations: Avoid setting unrealistic standards for yourself. Understand that it's okay to make mistakes and that failure is a stepping stone towards success.

e. Mindful Self-Compassion Breaks: Take short breaks throughout the day to practise mindfulness and self-compassion. Pause, take a few deep breaths, and offer yourself kind and supportive words.

5. Overcoming Resistance to Self-Compassion:

Embracing self-compassion can be challenging, especially if we have been conditioned to believe that self-criticism is necessary for personal growth. Recognize that self-compassion is not about avoiding responsibility or condoning harmful behaviours. It's about acknowledging our humanness and treating ourselves with the care we deserve.

Practising self-compassion and reducing self-criticism are transformative practices that can lead to a deeper sense of well-being and contentment. By treating ourselves with kindness and understanding, we can create a foundation of inner strength and resilience, ultimately enabling us to live a good life filled with joy and fulfilment. Remember, self-compassion is a skill that can be cultivated over time with patience and dedication to nurturing a positive and loving relationship with yourself.

Mindful Living for Enhanced Well-Being and Inner Peace

Mindfulness, the practice of being fully present and aware of the present moment, has gained significant attention in recent years for its profound impact on mental and emotional well-being. In these sections the concept of mindful living and how it can lead to enhanced well-being and inner peace.

I. Understanding Mindful Living

Mindful living is about consciously choosing to be fully engaged and attentive to the present moment without judgement. It involves paying deliberate attention to our thoughts, feelings, bodily sensations, and the environment around us. The essence of mindful living lies in being present with our experiences, no matter how ordinary or extraordinary they may be.

A. Cultivating Mindfulness Practices

1. Mindful Breathing: We'll explore the practice of focusing on our breath as a way to anchor our awareness in the present moment. Through mindful breathing, we can calm the mind, reduce stress, and

increase our ability to respond thoughtfully to life's challenges.

2. Body Scan Meditation: This practice involves systematically scanning through the body, paying attention to each sensation without trying to change anything. By doing so, we develop a deeper connection with our physical self and cultivate a greater sense of body awareness.

3. Mindful Eating: We'll discuss how to savour and fully experience each bite of food, fostering a healthier relationship with eating. Mindful eating encourages us to be aware of hunger and satiety cues, leading to a more balanced approach to nourishing our bodies.

II. The Benefits of Mindful Living

A. Stress Reduction and Emotional Regulation

1. Reducing Stress: Mindful living allows us to respond to stressors with greater clarity and calmness. By acknowledging our thoughts and emotions without judgement, we can prevent stress from escalating and negatively impacting our well-being.

2. Emotion Regulation: Through mindfulness, we become more attuned to our emotions and learn to navigate them with self-compassion. This helps us handle challenging emotions such as anxiety, anger, and sadness more effectively.

B. Improved Mental Clarity and Focus

1. Enhanced Concentration: The practice of mindfulness enhances our ability to focus on tasks and activities, promoting productivity and creativity.

2. Clearing Mental Clutter: We'll explore how mindfulness helps us recognize and detach from distracting thoughts, allowing

mental space for clarity and a greater sense
of purpose.

III. Mindful Communication and
Relationships

A. Active Listening: Mindful communication
involves truly listening to others without
interruption or judgement. By giving our full
attention to the speaker, we foster deeper
connections and understanding in our
relationships.

B. Empathy and Compassion: Practising
mindfulness enhances our capacity for
empathy and compassion, allowing us to
relate to others with kindness and
understanding.

IV. Cultivating Self-Compassion

A. Treating Ourselves with Kindness: We'll
discuss the importance of self-compassion

and the practice of being as kind to ourselves as we are to our loved ones.

B. Overcoming Self-Criticism: Mindful living helps us identify and transform self-critical thoughts into more supportive and nurturing ones.

C. Embracing Imperfections: We'll explore how mindfulness allows us to accept our imperfections and embrace our humanity with a sense of self-acceptance and love.

V. Mindfulness in Daily Life

A. Bringing Mindfulness to Routine Activities: We'll discuss how to incorporate mindfulness into everyday tasks like washing dishes, walking, or commuting, transforming mundane moments into opportunities for peace and presence.

B. Mindful Technology Use: We'll address the impact of constant digital distractions and explore strategies to use technology more mindfully for greater well-being.

VI. Mindful Living and Inner Peace

A. Embracing Stillness: Mindful living opens doors to inner peace by cultivating a sense of stillness amidst life's busyness.

B. Letting Go of Attachments: We'll explore how mindfulness encourages us to detach from unnecessary attachments and find contentment in the present moment.

Mindful living is a transformative journey that empowers us to find inner peace, reduce stress, and cultivate a deeper connection with ourselves and others. By integrating mindfulness practices into our daily lives, we can enhance our well-being and lead a more fulfilling and meaningful existence. The path to inner peace begins with the simple act of being fully

present—embracing the joy within each
moment.

Chapter 6: Balancing Work, Life, and Leisure

Strategies for Achieving Work-Life Balance

In today's fast-paced and demanding world, finding a harmonious balance between work and personal life has become a paramount challenge for many individuals. The pressures of modern society often lead to overwhelming workloads, extended working hours, and little time left for personal pursuits and leisure activities. However, achieving a healthy work-life balance is not only crucial for our overall well-being but also plays a significant role in enhancing productivity and job satisfaction.

1. Assessing Your Current Work-Life Balance:

The first step towards achieving a better work-life balance is self-awareness. Take some time to assess your current situation honestly. Reflect on how much time you spend at work, the demands of your job, and the impact it has on your personal life. Are you consistently sacrificing personal time for work-related commitments? Identifying areas of imbalance will allow you to make more informed decisions moving forward.

2. Set Clear Boundaries:

Establishing clear boundaries between work and personal life is essential for maintaining balance. Define specific working hours and stick to them whenever possible. Communicate these boundaries to colleagues, superiors, and clients, so they are aware of your availability. By doing so, you can create a structure that respects both your work commitments and personal time.

3. Prioritise Tasks and Delegate:

Effective time management is key to achieving work-life balance. Prioritise tasks based on their importance and urgency. Focus on completing high-priority assignments during designated work hours, and if possible, delegate less critical tasks to colleagues or team members. By delegating responsibility, you can alleviate some of the workload pressure and create space for personal pursuits.

4. Utilise Technology Wisely:

While technology has undoubtedly improved work efficiency, it can also blur the lines between work and personal life. Establish guidelines for technology usage outside of work hours. Avoid checking work emails or taking business calls during designated personal time. Disconnecting from work-related technology will allow you to recharge and fully engage in leisure activities.

5. Schedule Regular Breaks:

Incorporating regular breaks into your workday can significantly impact your productivity and well-being. Take short breaks throughout the day to rest and recharge. Utilise this time for stretching, meditating, or going for a short walk. Stepping away from work temporarily can enhance focus and creativity when you return to your tasks.

6. Create a Supportive Work Environment:

An inclusive and supportive work environment can positively influence work-life balance. Encourage open communication with colleagues and supervisors about your work-life needs. Many companies are increasingly recognizing the importance of work-life balance and implementing flexible policies

that accommodate their employees'
well-being.

7. Learn to Say No:

It can be challenging to say no to additional
work tasks or commitments, but setting
boundaries is vital for maintaining work-life
balance. If taking on extra responsibilities
will jeopardise your personal time or
well-being, politely decline or negotiate a
more manageable workload.

8. Invest in Self-Care:

Nurturing yourself physically, emotionally,
and mentally is essential for achieving
work-life balance. Make time for self-care
activities that bring you joy and relaxation.
Engage in hobbies, exercise, practice
mindfulness, or spend quality time with
loved ones. By prioritising self-care, you'll
be better equipped to handle the challenges
of both work and personal life.

Striving for work-life balance is a journey that requires continuous effort and adaptation. Implementing the strategies discussed in this section can empower you to reclaim control over your time, find harmony between work and personal life, and ultimately lead a more fulfilling and satisfying lifestyle. Remember that achieving balance is not about perfection but about making conscious choices that align with your values and well-being. In the next section, we will explore how to incorporate leisure and hobbies into your daily routine to further enhance your work-life balance.

Incorporating Leisure and Hobbies into Daily Routines

In the pursuit of a balanced and fulfilling life, incorporating leisure and hobbies into our daily routines plays a crucial role. Many of us lead busy lives filled with responsibilities and commitments, leaving little time for ourselves and the activities that bring us joy. However, making time for leisure and hobbies is essential for our well-being, creativity, and overall happiness.

1. The Importance of Leisure and Hobbies:
   At the core of embracing the joy within is the recognition that leisure and hobbies are not mere indulgences but vital components of a healthy lifestyle. Engaging in activities we enjoy helps to reduce stress, improve mental health, and increase overall life satisfaction. Hobbies provide a space for self-expression and creativity, allowing us to explore our passions and interests outside of our regular responsibilities.

2. Identifying Personal Leisure Activities and Hobbies:
   Begin by identifying leisure activities and hobbies that resonate with you. Reflect on

past interests or consider trying out new activities that intrigue you. Whether it's painting, playing a musical instrument, gardening, hiking, cooking, or simply reading a book, find activities that bring you a sense of fulfilment and relaxation.

3. Time Management for Leisure:
   Balancing work, life, and leisure requires effective time management. Schedule dedicated blocks of time for your chosen leisure activities and hobbies. This may mean setting aside a few hours each week or even short daily intervals to engage in these pursuits. Treat these time slots as non-negotiable and prioritise them just as you would with any other important commitment.

4. Creating a Leisure-Friendly Environment:
   Foster an environment that encourages and supports your leisure activities and hobbies. Set up a designated space in your home where you can pursue your interests

without distractions. Whether it's a cosy corner for reading or a well-lit studio for crafting, having a dedicated space enhances the enjoyment and consistency of your leisure pursuits.

5. Exploring New Hobbies and Activities:
   As we grow and evolve, our interests may change. Embrace the opportunity to explore new hobbies and activities that pique your curiosity. Trying new things not only keeps life exciting but also opens doors to new experiences and potential passions you never knew existed.

6. Engaging in Leisure Activities with Others:
   While some hobbies can be solitary, consider participating in leisure activities with friends, family, or like-minded individuals. Joining clubs, classes, or online communities centred around your interests can provide a sense of camaraderie and deepen your enjoyment of the activity.

7. Balancing Screen Time and Digital
Leisure:

In the digital age, it's essential to be
mindful of screen time and its potential
impact on our leisure activities. While
technology can enhance certain hobbies and
provide opportunities for connection,
excessive screen time may detract from the
quality of our leisure experiences. Set
boundaries and prioritise face-to-face
interactions and activities that allow you to
disconnect from screens.

8. Overcoming Barriers to Leisure:

It's common to encounter obstacles that
hinder our ability to engage in leisure
activities regularly. Whether it's
work-related stress, family commitments, or
personal challenges, identify these barriers
and develop strategies to overcome them.
Time management, delegation, and setting
realistic expectations can help you navigate

these challenges and carve out time for leisure.

Incorporating leisure and hobbies into daily routines is a powerful way to nurture the joy within and find balance in our lives. By dedicating time to activities that bring us happiness, we can recharge, discover new aspects of ourselves, and cultivate a deeper sense of contentment. Remember, these leisure pursuits are not indulgent luxuries but essential components of a well-lived life. Embrace the joy they bring and cherish the moments of self-discovery and fulfilment they offer.

The Importance of Downtime and Relaxation for Overall Happiness

In our fast-paced and hectic lives, it's easy to get caught up in the daily grind of work and responsibilities. However, one vital aspect that often gets neglected is the significance of downtime and relaxation.

1. Recognizing the Need for Downtime:
  The first step in understanding the importance of downtime is recognizing its necessity. Our bodies and minds are not designed to be in a constant state of productivity and stress. Without adequate breaks and moments of relaxation, we risk burnout and diminishing our overall sense of happiness.

2. The Benefits of Downtime:
  Downtime is not merely a luxury; it is a fundamental need for our mental and physical health. Taking time to relax allows our minds to decompress, recharge, and process the events of the day. It can enhance creativity, problem-solving skills, and decision-making abilities. Moreover, downtime provides an opportunity for our bodies to recover, reducing the risk of stress-related illnesses.

3. Different Forms of Relaxation:
    Relaxation can take many forms, and what works best for one person may not be suitable for another. It's essential to explore various relaxation techniques and find what resonates with you. Some may find solace in meditation, yoga, or deep breathing exercises, while others may prefer engaging in hobbies, spending time in nature, or listening to music.

4. Incorporating Downtime into Daily Life:
    Creating a habit of downtime is crucial for sustaining happiness in the long term. It's essential to set aside dedicated time each day for relaxation, even if it's just a few minutes. This can be done during breaks at work, before going to bed, or as part of a morning routine. By making relaxation a regular practice, we prioritise our well-being and ensure a healthy work-life balance.

5. Disconnecting from Technology:

In our modern digital age, technology has become an integral part of our lives. While it brings convenience, it also has the potential to add stress and disrupt our downtime. Learning to disconnect from technology during relaxation periods can be immensely beneficial. Consider setting boundaries for smartphone use, avoiding work-related emails during personal time, and embracing tech-free activities.

6. The Link between Relaxation and Productivity:
Contrary to popular belief, taking breaks and engaging in downtime can boost productivity. Studies have shown that individuals who incorporate regular relaxation into their routines are more focused, energised, and efficient during their active hours. It allows the brain to reset, leading to improved concentration and enhanced cognitive abilities.

7. Strategies for Effective Relaxation:

For some, the concept of relaxation may be challenging to grasp, especially for those accustomed to a busy lifestyle. Implementing relaxation strategies may require patience and practice. Consider setting realistic goals for downtime, seeking support from friends or family, or even joining relaxation classes to discover what works best for you.

8. The Power of Restorative Sleep:
Quality sleep is an integral part of relaxation and overall happiness. Getting enough restorative sleep is essential for physical and mental rejuvenation. Establishing healthy sleep habits and a relaxing bedtime routine can significantly impact overall well-being and happiness.

The importance of downtime and relaxation cannot be overstated. Taking the time to unwind, decompress, and engage in activities that bring joy and peace can profoundly influence our overall happiness and life satisfaction. By incorporating regular downtime into our lives, we create a healthier work-life balance, improve productivity, and cultivate a greater sense of well-being. Embracing the power of relaxation is a step toward living a more fulfilling and joyous life.

Chapter 7: Grappling with Adversity and Resilience

Coping with Life's Challenges and Setbacks

Life is an ever-changing journey filled with both joys and hardships. Challenges and setbacks are inevitable, but how we respond to them plays a pivotal role in our overall well-being and happiness.

1. Understanding the Nature of Challenges:

Life's challenges come in various forms – from personal struggles to external circumstances beyond our control. It is essential to recognize that adversity is a natural part of the human experience. By accepting this reality, we can better prepare ourselves to face life's trials with a more open and adaptable mindset.

2. Cultivating Emotional Awareness:

When faced with challenges, it is common to experience a wide range of emotions such as fear, anger, sadness, or frustration. Cultivating emotional awareness allows us to acknowledge and understand these feelings without judgement. By embracing our emotions, we create space for healing and growth.

3. Building a Support System:

One of the most valuable resources during tough times is a strong support system. Surrounding ourselves with caring and understanding individuals – family, friends, or support groups – can provide comfort, encouragement, and perspective. Sharing our challenges with others can alleviate the burden and help us see different solutions.

4. Practising Mindfulness in Adversity:

Mindfulness, the practice of being fully present in the moment without judgement, can be a powerful tool in navigating through challenges. By cultivating mindfulness, we learn to observe our thoughts and reactions, allowing us to respond to adversity with greater clarity and composure.

5. Embracing a Growth Mindset:

Adopting a growth mindset means viewing challenges as opportunities for learning and personal development. Instead of seeing setbacks as failures, we can reframe them as stepping stones towards growth. Embracing a growth mindset empowers us to bounce back stronger and more resilient than before.

6. Fostering Adaptability and Flexibility:

Life's challenges often require us to adapt to new circumstances and embrace change.

Cultivating adaptability and flexibility helps us navigate uncharted waters with grace and confidence. Embracing change as a natural part of life allows us to approach challenges with a sense of curiosity and openness.

7. Seeking Professional Help When Needed:

Sometimes, life's challenges may be too overwhelming to handle on our own. Seeking support from professional counsellors or therapists can provide valuable insights and coping strategies. There is no shame in reaching out for help when it is necessary, as it is a sign of strength and self-awareness.

8. Practising Self-Compassion:

During difficult times, it is crucial to be kind and compassionate to ourselves. Self-compassion involves treating ourselves with the same understanding and care we would offer to a friend facing challenges. By practising self-compassion, we cultivate resilience and foster a sense of inner strength.

9. Learning from Past Resilience:

Reflecting on past experiences where we demonstrated resilience can serve as a reminder of our inner strength. Recalling how we successfully navigated through challenging situations can boost our confidence in facing current adversities.

10. Embracing Patience and Endurance:

Coping with life's challenges often requires patience and endurance. Resilience is not about bouncing back immediately; it is a process of gradual healing and growth. Embracing patience allows us to give ourselves the time and space needed to recover and rebuild.

Coping with life's challenges and setbacks is an integral part of the human experience. By understanding the nature of challenges, cultivating emotional awareness, building a support system, and practising mindfulness, we can navigate through difficult times with greater resilience and inner strength. Embracing a growth mindset, fostering adaptability, seeking professional help when needed, and practising self-compassion are all essential components of building resilience. Remember, each challenge presents an opportunity for growth, and by embracing the journey, we can emerge stronger and more capable of leading a good life filled with joy and fulfilment.

Building Resilience and Bouncing Back from Difficulties

Life is a journey filled with ups and downs, challenges, and triumphs. Resilience is not about avoiding difficulties; rather, it's about developing the capacity to face them head-on, adapt, and grow through life's inevitable obstacles.

Understanding Resilience: The Power of Adaptation

Resilience is often compared to the ability of a tree to bend with the wind and then stand tall again once the storm passes. It is the psychological and emotional flexibility that allows individuals to face adversities, setbacks, or traumatic experiences without being overwhelmed. Resilience does not mean that we are immune to pain or hardship; instead, it enables us to cope and recover in a healthy way.

Recognizing Resilient Traits

Resilience is not a fixed trait; rather, it is a set of skills and attitudes that can be cultivated and strengthened over time. It is crucial to recognize the characteristics of resilient individuals to better understand how to build resilience within ourselves:

1. Positive Outlook: Resilient individuals maintain a positive perspective, focusing on the possibilities for growth and learning even in challenging situations. They see setbacks as temporary and embrace a sense of optimism for the future.

2. Adaptive Thinking: They are adaptable and open to change. Resilient people understand that life is dynamic, and they are willing to adjust their strategies and perspectives as needed.

3. Problem-Solving Skills: Resilient individuals approach problems with a solution-oriented mindset. They seek creative ways to overcome obstacles and find effective ways to navigate difficulties.

4. Emotional Regulation: Building resilience involves managing emotions effectively.

Resilient individuals allow themselves to feel their emotions without getting overwhelmed by them, allowing for healthy emotional processing.

5. Social Support: A strong support network is vital for resilience. Resilient individuals foster positive relationships and lean on their support system during challenging times.

Building Resilience: Strategies and Techniques

1. Cultivating a Growth Mindset: Embracing a growth mindset is foundational to building resilience. Understand that challenges and failures are opportunities for learning and personal development. When we view setbacks as stepping stones, we are better equipped to adapt and grow.

2. Developing Coping Mechanisms: Identify healthy coping mechanisms that work for

you. These may include exercise, meditation, journaling, or engaging in hobbies that bring joy. Building a toolkit of coping strategies helps you manage stress effectively.

3. Learning from Past Experiences: Reflect on past challenges and how you overcame them. What strategies were successful, and what can be improved? This self-awareness can provide valuable insights for future resilience.

4. Building a Support Network: Nurture meaningful connections with friends, family, or support groups. Having a reliable support network provides comfort during tough times and can offer valuable perspectives and advice.

5. Practising Self-Compassion: Be kind to yourself during challenging moments. Acknowledge that everyone faces hardships, and it's okay to experience emotions. Treat

yourself with the same understanding and compassion you would offer a friend.

6. Setting Realistic Goals: Establish attainable goals and milestones. Celebrate each accomplishment, no matter how small, as it reinforces your sense of progress and achievement.

Overcoming Obstacles with Resilience

Life's adversities come in various forms – loss, failure, rejection, or unexpected changes. Resilience empowers us to face these obstacles with strength and courage. The key lies in maintaining a growth mindset, focusing on adaptive thinking, and actively applying the strategies and techniques mentioned above.

Resilience is not developed overnight; it requires continuous practice and effort. Embrace challenges as opportunities to strengthen your resilience muscle. By doing so, you'll discover that adversity becomes a catalyst for personal growth, and you'll bounce back from difficulties with newfound wisdom and strength.

Transforming Adversity into Opportunities for Growth

Life is full of challenges and adversities, and no one is immune to facing difficulties. This section explores the concept of transforming adversity into opportunities for growth, recognizing that every setback can be a stepping stone to personal development and resilience.

1. Embracing the Power of Perception

How we perceive and interpret adversities can significantly impact our ability to overcome them. Instead of viewing challenges as roadblocks, we can shift our mindset to see them as opportunities for growth and learning. By embracing a positive and growth-oriented perspective, we open ourselves up to new possibilities and solutions.

2. Practising Self-Reflection

When faced with adversity, taking time for self-reflection can be incredibly valuable. Self-reflection allows us to gain insights into our thoughts, emotions, and reactions, enabling us to understand how we handle challenges. By examining our responses to difficult situations, we can identify patterns, strengths, and areas for improvement, fostering personal growth.

3. Cultivating Resilience

Resilience is the ability to bounce back and adapt in the face of adversity. Building resilience involves developing coping mechanisms and a strong support system.

We can cultivate resilience by nurturing our emotional well-being, maintaining healthy relationships, and seeking support from friends, family, or professionals when needed.

4. Embracing Change and Flexibility

Adversity often comes hand in hand with change. Embracing change and staying flexible allow us to navigate challenges more effectively. By being open to new possibilities and adjusting our approaches, we can find creative solutions and opportunities for growth even in the face of uncertainty.

5. Learning from Adversity

Every adversity provides a chance to learn valuable lessons. Whether it's a setback in our career, a personal struggle, or a difficult life event, reflecting on the experience can yield profound insights. Learning from adversity can lead to personal growth, increased self-awareness, and the development of problem-solving skills.

6. Seeking Support and Connection

During challenging times, seeking support and connection with others is essential. Sharing our struggles with trusted friends, family members, or support groups can provide emotional relief and practical advice. Knowing that we are not alone in our adversities can help us navigate through them more effectively.

7. Emphasising the Power of Adaptability

Adaptability is a key attribute in transforming adversity into opportunities for growth. Life is dynamic and ever-changing, and our ability to adapt to new circumstances can determine our success in turning challenges into positive outcomes. Being adaptable allows us to respond effectively to unexpected situations and find innovative solutions.

8. Setting Realistic Goals

When facing adversity, setting realistic and achievable goals can provide direction and motivation. By breaking down larger challenges into smaller, manageable steps, we can approach difficulties with a sense of purpose and accomplishment as we make progress toward overcoming them.

9. Practising Self-Compassion

Throughout the process of grappling with adversity, it's crucial to practise self-compassion. Treating ourselves with kindness and understanding during difficult times allows us to maintain a healthy self-image and cope with stress more effectively. Self-compassion enables us to be gentle with ourselves as we work through challenges, fostering a positive mindset for growth.

10. Celebrating Progress and Successes

As we transform adversity into opportunities for growth, it's essential to celebrate our progress and successes, no matter how small they may seem. Recognizing our efforts and achievements along the way reinforces a sense of accomplishment and encourages us to keep moving forward with resilience and determination.

Transforming adversity into opportunities for growth is a powerful mindset that empowers us to face life's challenges with resilience and optimism. By embracing the power of perception, practising self-reflection, cultivating resilience, and embracing change, we can harness the potential within adversities to foster personal growth and a greater sense of fulfilment in our lives. Through learning, seeking support, emphasising adaptability, and setting realistic goals, we can navigate through difficulties with grace and strength, ultimately finding opportunities for growth even in the most challenging circumstances. Remember that self-compassion and celebrating progress are essential components in this transformative journey, as they allow us to approach adversities with kindness and appreciation for the growth they bring.

Chapter 8: Embracing Change and Letting Go

Embracing Change as a Natural Part of Life

Change is an inevitable and constant part of life. From the moment we are born, we experience an ever-evolving world that shapes and moulds us. Yet, despite its inevitability, many of us find ourselves resisting change, holding on to familiar routines and comfort zones. This section will explore the concept of change as a natural part of life and how embracing it can lead to personal growth, resilience, and a deeper sense of fulfilment.

1. The Nature of Change

Change is woven into the very fabric of existence. Seasons shift, flowers bloom and wither, and day turns into night. As humans, we are not exempt from this universal law of impermanence. Our lives are marked by a series of transitions, both major and minor. From childhood to adolescence, adulthood to old age, and the myriad experiences in between, change is an ever-present companion on our journey.

2. The Fear of the Unknown

One of the primary reasons we resist change is the fear of the unknown. Stepping into uncharted territory can be daunting and unsettling. It triggers feelings of uncertainty, vulnerability, and anxiety. Our minds tend to cling to what is familiar, even if it no longer serves us, as a way to protect ourselves from the uncertainties of the future. However, when we recognize that change is unavoidable, we can learn to navigate it with grace and courage.

3. Embracing Change as an Opportunity

Embracing change opens the door to endless opportunities for growth and self-discovery. When we let go of resistance and accept change as a natural part of life, we create space for new experiences, perspectives, and possibilities. Each change, whether positive or challenging, presents an opportunity to learn, adapt, and evolve.

4. The Power of Adaptability

Adaptability is a key trait that enables us to thrive in a rapidly changing world. Just like a tree bends with the wind, our ability to adapt allows us to face life's challenges with resilience. Embracing change cultivates our adaptability, empowering us to respond to unforeseen circumstances with creativity and resourcefulness.

5. Embracing Change as a Catalyst for Personal Growth

Personal growth often occurs when we step outside our comfort zones and embrace change. Whether it's starting a new job, moving to a different city, or ending a long-term relationship, each change nudges us toward self-discovery and self-awareness. The process of adapting to change forces us to examine our beliefs, values, and priorities, leading to profound inner transformations.

6. Letting Go of Attachments

To embrace change fully, we must be willing to let go of attachments to the past or expectations for the future. Holding on to what was or what could be can hinder our ability to fully experience the present moment. By releasing our grip on the past, we free ourselves to savour the beauty of the present and embrace the possibilities of the future.

7. Finding Balance in Change

While embracing change is crucial for personal growth, it's also essential to find balance and avoid overwhelming ourselves with constant upheaval. Change can be both invigorating and exhausting, so it's essential to practise self-care and mindfulness during times of transition. Nurturing ourselves through change allows us to navigate it with grace and poise.

Change is an integral part of the human experience. By embracing it as a natural aspect of life, we can harness its transformative power and embrace personal growth and resilience. Embracing change enables us to let go of fear and attachments, opening ourselves to new opportunities and possibilities. When we accept change as a constant companion, we can navigate life's twists and turns with grace, curiosity, and a profound sense of empowerment.

Techniques for Coping with Transitions and Uncertainty

In life, change is inevitable. Whether it's a major life transition or smaller everyday shifts, navigating uncertainty can be challenging. However, it is possible to build resilience and embrace change with grace. This section will explore various techniques that can help individuals cope with transitions and uncertainty, enabling them to thrive even in the face of ambiguity.

1. Acknowledge and Accept the Reality of Change:
   The first step in coping with transitions and uncertainty is acknowledging that change is a natural part of life. Resisting or denying change can create unnecessary

stress and anxiety. Instead, practise acceptance and recognize that change presents opportunities for growth and new experiences.

2. Develop a Growth Mindset:
   Cultivate a growth mindset that views challenges and setbacks as opportunities to learn and improve. Embrace the belief that you can adapt and grow through change, rather than being limited by it. This mindset shift empowers you to face uncertainties with optimism and resilience.

3. Seek Support and Communication:
   During times of change and uncertainty, seeking support from friends, family, or a professional counsellor can be immensely helpful. Talking about your feelings and concerns with someone you trust can provide comfort and perspective, reducing feelings of isolation.

4. Stay Present with Mindfulness:

Practising mindfulness can anchor you in the present moment and reduce anxiety about the unknown future. Engage in mindfulness techniques, such as meditation and deep breathing, to stay centred and calm amidst change.

5. Focus on What You Can Control:
In uncertain times, it's easy to feel overwhelmed by the vastness of change. Focus on what you can control rather than fixating on what you can't. By directing your energy towards actionable steps, you'll gain a sense of empowerment and purpose.

6. Embrace Flexibility and Adaptability:
Rigidity can make change feel daunting. Embrace flexibility and adaptability as essential skills for navigating uncertainty. Be open to adjusting your plans and expectations as circumstances evolve.

7. Set Realistic Expectations:

Understand that coping with transitions takes time and effort. Set realistic expectations for yourself and others during periods of change. Give yourself permission to experience a range of emotions, recognizing that healing and growth occur at different paces.

8. Emphasise Self-Care:
   Taking care of yourself physically, emotionally, and mentally is crucial during times of uncertainty. Prioritise self-care activities that nourish your well-being, such as exercise, healthy eating, creative pursuits, and relaxation.

9. Visualise Positive Outcomes:
   Redirect your focus from potential negative outcomes to visualising positive possibilities. Visualising a favourable future can instil hope and motivation to take proactive steps towards creating that reality.

10. Learn from Past Experiences:

Reflect on how you've successfully navigated past changes in your life. Draw upon those experiences to remind yourself of your resilience and adaptability. Recognize that you have the inner strength to handle whatever comes your way.

11. Practice Gratitude:
Gratitude can be a powerful antidote to fear and uncertainty. Cultivate a daily gratitude practice by acknowledging the blessings and positive aspects of your life. Gratitude fosters a sense of contentment and helps shift your focus from fear to abundance.

12. Embrace the Journey:
Change is an ongoing process, and life's journey is full of twists and turns. Embrace the journey, including its uncertainties, as an opportunity for growth, learning, and self-discovery. View change as a chance to evolve into the best version of yourself.

By incorporating these techniques into your life, you'll be better equipped to cope with transitions and uncertainties. Remember that embracing change and letting go is not about suppressing emotions but allowing yourself to adapt and thrive in the face of life's inevitable transformations. Embrace each moment as an opportunity to grow, learn, and uncover the hidden potential within yourself.

The Art of Letting Go and Moving Forward with Positivity

Letting go is often one of the most challenging aspects of embracing change and living a good life. It involves releasing attachments to the past, relinquishing control over things beyond our reach, and accepting that life is a continuous journey of growth and transformation.

1. Acknowledging Resistance to Change:

Letting go can be difficult because it requires us to confront our fears and uncertainties about the unknown. We might find ourselves clinging to familiar routines, relationships, or beliefs, even if they no longer serve our growth and well-being. Understanding and acknowledging this resistance is the first step in the process of letting go.

2. Embracing Impermanence:
Life is inherently impermanent, and change is the only constant. Embracing the idea that everything has its season can help us become more adaptable and open to new experiences. Rather than holding on tightly to what was, we can appreciate each moment for what it offers and gracefully let go when it's time to move on.

3. Releasing Attachments:
Attachments to people, possessions, or outcomes can create emotional burdens and limit our ability to move forward. Learning

to detach ourselves from the need for
specific outcomes allows us to free ourselves
from the weight of expectations and open up
to new possibilities.

4. Forgiving and Healing:
  Letting go often involves forgiving
ourselves and others for past mistakes and
hurtful experiences. By releasing
resentments and grudges, we can heal
emotional wounds and create space for
positivity and growth in our lives.

5. Practising Mindfulness:
  Mindfulness is a powerful tool in the
process of letting go. Being present in the
moment and non-judgmentally observing
our thoughts and emotions helps us become
aware of what we are holding on to and
enables us to release negative patterns.

6. Gratitude and Acceptance:
  Cultivating gratitude for the past and
acceptance of the present allows us to let go

with a sense of peace and contentment.
Even if certain experiences were
challenging, they have contributed to who
we are today and have valuable lessons to
teach us.

7. Moving Forward with Purpose:
   Letting go is not about forgetting the past,
but rather, integrating its lessons into our
journey forward. Setting clear intentions
and goals for the future helps us channel our
energy and focus toward positive growth
and meaningful achievements.

8. Building Resilience:
   Embracing change and letting go require
resilience. Developing resilience involves
nurturing our inner strength and coping
skills, which enable us to bounce back from
setbacks and navigate new challenges with
courage and determination.

9. Seeking Support:

Letting go can be an emotional process, and seeking support from friends, family, or professional counsellors can be beneficial. Sharing our feelings and experiences with others can provide valuable insights and encouragement as we navigate this transformative journey.

10. Embracing the New:
As we let go of the old, we create space for new opportunities and experiences to enter our lives. Embracing the unknown with a positive and open mindset allows us to welcome fresh perspectives and embrace change as a catalyst for growth and self-discovery.

The art of letting go is a transformative practice that empowers us to move forward with positivity, resilience, and a sense of purpose. By acknowledging resistance, embracing impermanence, and releasing attachments, we can navigate change with grace and gratitude. Mindfulness, forgiveness, and seeking support help us heal and grow as we embrace new beginnings. By letting go of what no longer serves us, we open ourselves to the endless possibilities that life has to offer. Letting go becomes an empowering choice, leading us towards living a good life filled with joy, fulfilment, and authentic happiness.

Chapter 9: Living a Healthy and Balanced Lifestyle

The Connection Between Physical Health and Emotional Well-being

This section will delve into the profound interrelation between physical health and emotional well-being. It is no secret that our bodies and minds are intricately connected, and nurturing one aspect positively impacts the other. Understanding this correlation is pivotal in our quest for a good life filled with joy and fulfilment. Through comprehensive lifestyle choices, we can foster optimal physical health, leading to enhanced emotional resilience and overall well-being.

The Influence of Physical Health on Emotional Well-being:

Our physical health exerts a profound impact on our emotional state. When we are physically healthy, we tend to experience increased energy levels, reduced stress, and improved cognitive function. Regular physical activity, such as exercise and outdoor activities, releases endorphins, commonly known as "feel-good" hormones. These endorphins act as natural mood lifters, reducing feelings of anxiety, depression, and stress.

Furthermore, maintaining a balanced diet rich in essential nutrients and vitamins supports brain health and emotional stability. Nutrient-dense foods fuel our bodies and minds, optimising cognitive function and promoting emotional resilience.

Physical health also influences our sleep patterns, which significantly affect emotional well-being. Sufficient, restful sleep is crucial for emotional regulation and mental clarity. A well-rested mind is better equipped to handle challenges and process emotions effectively.

Strategies for Improving Physical Health:

1. Regular Exercise:
Engaging in regular physical activity is paramount for overall health and emotional well-being. Aim for at least 150 minutes of moderate-intensity exercise or 75 minutes of vigorous-intensity exercise per week. This can include activities such as walking, jogging, swimming, or yoga. Find activities that you enjoy to make it a sustainable part of your routine.

2. Balanced Nutrition:
Adopting a balanced and nutritious diet is essential for maintaining physical health. Incorporate a variety of fruits, vegetables, whole grains, lean proteins, and healthy fats into your meals. Limit the intake of processed and sugary foods, which can

negatively impact both physical and emotional health.

3. Prioritise Sleep:
Establish a consistent sleep schedule and create a calming bedtime routine to improve the quality of your sleep. Aim for 7-9 hours of sleep each night to promote emotional well-being and cognitive function.

4. Manage Stress:
Stress can take a toll on both physical and emotional health. Practice stress-reducing techniques such as meditation, deep breathing exercises, or spending time in nature. Engaging in hobbies and activities that bring joy and relaxation can also help alleviate stress.

The Influence of Emotional Well-being on Physical Health:

Just as physical health affects emotional well-being, the inverse is also true. Our emotional state impacts our physical health in profound ways. Chronic stress, anxiety, and negative emotions can manifest in physical symptoms and weaken the immune system, making us more susceptible to illness.

Emotional well-being plays a vital role in our ability to cope with life's challenges and navigate difficult situations. A positive emotional outlook fosters resilience, which is essential for adapting to change and bouncing back from adversity.

Strategies for Improving Emotional Well-being:

1. Practice Mindfulness:
Mindfulness involves staying present in the moment and being aware of our thoughts and emotions without judgement. Engaging in mindfulness practices, such as meditation and mindfulness exercises, can help reduce anxiety and promote emotional balance.

2. Cultivate Positive Relationships:
Nurturing positive and supportive relationships can bolster emotional well-being. Surround yourself with people who uplift and inspire you. Engage in meaningful conversations and seek emotional support when needed.

3. Practice Self-Compassion:
Be kind to yourself and practice self-compassion. Acknowledge your emotions without judgement and avoid self-criticism. Treat yourself with the same care and understanding you would offer a close friend.

4. Seek Professional Help if Needed:
If you find it challenging to manage your emotions or cope with stress, don't hesitate to seek support from a mental health professional. Therapy or counselling can provide valuable tools for emotional growth and well-being.

The intricate connection between physical health and emotional well-being underscores the importance of prioritising both aspects in our lives. By making conscious lifestyle choices that promote physical health and emotional well-being, we equip ourselves with the tools to lead a good life filled with joy and contentment. In the next section, we will explore the concept of mindfulness and self-compassion as powerful practices for nurturing emotional well-being.

Incorporating Exercise, Nutrition, and Rest into Daily Life

Living a healthy and balanced lifestyle involves nurturing our bodies and minds through proper exercise, nutrition, and rest. These fundamental aspects form the foundation of our overall well-being, contributing to our physical vitality and mental clarity.

The Power of Regular Exercise

Regular exercise is not just about attaining a certain body shape; it's a holistic practice that positively impacts various aspects of our health. From boosting cardiovascular fitness to improving mood and reducing stress, exercise is a potent tool for achieving optimal well-being.

A. Physical Benefits of Exercise

1. Improved Cardiovascular Health: Engaging in cardiovascular exercises such as running, cycling, or swimming strengthens the heart, improves blood circulation, and lowers the risk of heart disease.

2. Enhanced Muscle Strength and Flexibility: Resistance training and stretching exercises promote muscle growth

and flexibility, supporting better posture and reducing the risk of injuries.

3. Weight Management: Combining a balanced diet with regular physical activity helps in maintaining a healthy weight, reducing the risk of obesity-related conditions.

B. Mental and Emotional Benefits of Exercise

1. Stress Reduction: Physical activity triggers the release of endorphins, which are natural mood elevators, reducing stress and anxiety levels.

2. Improved Cognitive Function: Exercise has been linked to better cognitive function, memory retention, and mental clarity.

3. Boosted Self-Esteem: Regular exercise can enhance self-confidence and body image, promoting a positive self-perception.

II. Nourishing the Body with Proper Nutrition

Nutrition plays a pivotal role in supporting our physical health and well-being. Fueling our bodies with nutrient-dense foods provides the essential vitamins, minerals, and energy needed for optimal functioning.

A. The Importance of Balanced Nutrition

1. Whole Foods: Emphasising a diet rich in whole foods, such as fruits, vegetables, whole grains, lean proteins, and healthy fats, ensures a diverse array of nutrients.

2. Hydration: Staying adequately hydrated is crucial for various bodily functions, including digestion, temperature regulation, and nutrient transportation.

3. Mindful Eating: Practising mindful eating, being aware of hunger and fullness

cues, and savouring meals can lead to
healthier food choices and prevent
overeating.

B. Navigating Nutritional Challenges

1. Overcoming Emotional Eating:
Understanding the relationship between
emotions and food and finding alternative
ways to cope with emotional triggers.

2. Addressing Nutrient Deficiencies:
Identifying potential nutrient gaps and
incorporating supplements when necessary
under the guidance of healthcare
professionals.

III. The Importance of Quality Rest and
Sleep

In our fast-paced modern lives, sleep and
rest are often overlooked, yet they are
essential for restoring and rejuvenating our
bodies and minds.

A. The Role of Sleep in Health

1. Restorative Sleep: Quality sleep allows the body to repair tissues, consolidate memories, and regulate hormones, contributing to overall well-being.

2. Sleep and Mental Health: Lack of sleep can affect mood, cognitive function, and increase the risk of mental health issues like depression and anxiety.

B. Cultivating Healthy Sleep Habits

1. Creating a Sleep-Friendly Environment: Tips for optimising the sleep environment, including minimising light and noise disruptions and maintaining a comfortable temperature.

2. Establishing a Bedtime Routine: Developing consistent pre-sleep rituals to

signal the body that it's time to wind down and prepare for rest.

Incorporating regular exercise, balanced nutrition, and adequate rest into our daily lives is not just a short-term commitment but a lifelong journey towards improved well-being. By prioritising these elements and making conscious choices to care for our bodies and minds, we can achieve a sense of vitality and balance that enhances our overall quality of life.

Holistic Approaches to Maintaining a Healthy Lifestyle

Living a healthy and balanced lifestyle goes beyond just focusing on physical health; it encompasses the well-being of your mind, body, and spirit. Adopting holistic approaches can lead to overall wellness and a more fulfilling life. In this section, we will explore various facets of holistic health and the practices that can help you achieve a harmonious and vibrant existence.

1. Nourishing Nutrition:
  A vital aspect of holistic health is nourishing your body with the right nutrients. Opt for a balanced and diverse diet that includes a variety of fruits, vegetables, whole grains, lean proteins, and healthy fats. Aim to minimise processed and sugary foods, and choose natural, organic options whenever possible. Remember to stay hydrated by drinking plenty of water throughout the day, as proper hydration is crucial for maintaining bodily functions and overall well-being.

  It's also essential to listen to your body's unique needs. Pay attention to how different foods make you feel, and consider adopting an intuitive eating approach. Intuitive eating involves being mindful of hunger and fullness cues and eating in a way that honours your body's requirements without judgement or restriction.

2. Physical Activity and Movement:
   Regular physical activity is a cornerstone of holistic health. Engaging in exercise not only improves physical fitness but also has significant mental and emotional benefits. Find activities you enjoy, whether it's dancing, yoga, swimming, hiking, or simply going for a brisk walk. The key is to stay consistent and make movement an integral part of your daily routine.

   Additionally, incorporating movement throughout your day can make a substantial difference. Consider taking short breaks from sitting at your desk to stretch or do some light exercises. Embrace an active lifestyle by choosing the stairs over elevators, walking or cycling instead of driving short distances, and finding opportunities to move your body in fun and creative ways.

3. Managing Stress and Emotional
Well-Being:

Stress is an inevitable part of life, but
learning how to manage it effectively is
essential for holistic health. Chronic stress
can negatively impact both physical and
mental health, so it's crucial to find healthy
coping mechanisms.

Practising mindfulness and meditation can
be powerful tools for managing stress. These
practices help you become more aware of
your thoughts and emotions, allowing you to
respond to stressful situations with greater
clarity and calmness. Engage in
deep-breathing exercises, progressive
muscle relaxation, or guided imagery to
alleviate tension and promote relaxation.

Don't hesitate to seek support from
friends, family, or professional counsellors if
you find yourself overwhelmed. Talking
about your feelings and experiences can

provide a sense of relief and perspective, helping you navigate through challenging times.

4. Restorative Sleep:
  Sleep is a foundation of holistic health, as it allows your body and mind to rest, repair, and rejuvenate. Aim for seven to nine hours of quality sleep each night. Create a bedtime routine that promotes relaxation, such as reading a book, taking a warm bath, or practising gentle stretching before going to bed.

  Limit exposure to screens and stimulating activities close to bedtime, as these can interfere with your ability to fall asleep. Make your sleep environment comfortable and conducive to rest by keeping the room cool, dark, and quiet.

5. Connecting with Nature:
  Spending time in nature is a transformative practice for holistic health.

Nature offers a sense of peace and connectedness, and immersing yourself in natural surroundings can have profound effects on your well-being.

Make time for outdoor activities like hiking, picnics in the park, gardening, or simply taking a walk in a nearby green space. Disconnect from technology during these moments and fully embrace the beauty of nature. Even a short time spent outdoors can significantly boost your mood and reduce stress.

6. Embracing Holistic Therapies:
Holistic therapies can complement traditional medical practices and contribute to overall well-being. Explore alternative treatments like acupuncture, aromatherapy, massage therapy, and herbal remedies. These practices focus on balancing your body's energy and promoting harmony within.

When considering holistic therapies, consult with qualified practitioners and be open to exploring what resonates with you personally. These therapies can support your journey to holistic health and may offer unique benefits for your specific needs.

Incorporating holistic approaches into your lifestyle can lead to profound transformations in your overall health and well-being. By nourishing your body, mind, and spirit with intention and care, you'll find yourself on a path of self-discovery and a deeper connection to yourself and the world around you. Embrace these practices wholeheartedly, and you'll be well on your way to living a healthier, more balanced life filled with vitality and joy.

Chapter Ten: Spreading Joy and Kindness to Others

The Power of Giving Back and Acts of Kindness

In a world that can sometimes feel disconnected and fast-paced, the power of giving back and performing acts of kindness has the extraordinary ability to create ripples of joy and positivity in our lives and the lives of others. When we extend our compassion and selflessness to those around us, we not only make a positive impact on their well-being but also experience a profound sense of fulfilment and contentment within ourselves.

The Importance of Giving Back

Giving back to our communities and those in need is a vital aspect of living a good life. It provides us with an opportunity to contribute to the greater good and make a meaningful difference in the world. Whether it's volunteering at a local charity, donating to a cause we care about, or simply helping a neighbour in need, acts of giving back foster a sense of purpose and interconnectedness. Research has shown that engaging in altruistic activities can lead to increased happiness and reduced stress levels, contributing to an overall improved quality of life.

The Impact of Acts of Kindness
Acts of kindness, no matter how small, can have a profound impact on both the giver and the recipient. A genuine smile, a thoughtful gesture, or a helping hand can brighten someone's day and remind them that they are seen and valued. Moreover, acts of kindness have a contagious effect, inspiring others to pay it forward, creating a

chain reaction of positivity and compassion within communities. When we choose kindness, we foster an environment of empathy and understanding, making the world a better place one small act at a time.

Practising Random Acts of Kindness
One beautiful way to spread joy and kindness is by embracing the concept of "random acts of kindness." These are unexpected, selfless acts that bring positivity and warmth to someone's day. From leaving a kind note on a colleague's desk to paying for a stranger's coffee, the possibilities for random acts of kindness are limitless. Engaging in these acts not only brings joy to others but also nurtures a sense of purpose and connection within ourselves. Additionally, the element of surprise and delight associated with random acts of kindness creates lasting memories for both the giver and the recipient.

The Ripple Effect of Kindness

Just like a pebble dropped into a pond, acts of kindness create ripples that extend far beyond the initial action. When we spread kindness to others, we unknowingly inspire them to do the same. This ripple effect can reach far and wide, touching the lives of countless individuals. Imagine the collective impact we can make when each one of us chooses to be kind and compassionate towards others. The ripple effect of kindness has the potential to transform communities and foster a culture of caring and empathy.

Kindness towards Ourselves
While it is essential to spread kindness to others, it is equally important to extend that same kindness to ourselves. Often, we are our harshest critics, and self-compassion may be elusive. Embracing self-kindness involves treating ourselves with the same love, understanding, and forgiveness we would offer to a dear friend. By practising self-compassion, we create a strong foundation of emotional well-being,

enabling us to give back to others from a place of authenticity and genuine care.

Finding Opportunities for Giving Back
Integrating acts of kindness and giving back into our daily lives doesn't have to be complicated. Simple gestures can hold immense power. It could be as straightforward as holding the door for someone, offering a sincere compliment, or lending a listening ear to a friend in need. Engaging in community service, supporting local businesses, or participating in charitable events are other ways to make a difference. The key is to be mindful of the opportunities around us and to approach them with an open heart and a willingness to create positive change.

The power of giving back and acts of kindness lies in their ability to create a harmonious and compassionate society. As we spread joy and kindness to others, we foster a sense of unity and shared purpose, making the world a more beautiful and empathetic place to live. Remember, small acts of kindness can have a profound impact, not only on the recipients but on ourselves as well. Embrace the spirit of giving back, and let your acts of kindness be a beacon of light in a world that can always use more love and compassion.

Impacting Others Positively through Empathy and Compassion

In our quest for a good life, we often focus on personal growth and happiness, but we must not overlook the profound impact we can have on others through empathy and compassion. Understanding the emotions and experiences of those around us allows us to form genuine connections, offer support, and spread joy in meaningful ways. In this section, we will explore the power of empathy and compassion, how they contribute to a fulfilling life, and practical ways to cultivate these qualities in our interactions with others.

The Power of Empathy

Empathy is the ability to put ourselves in someone else's shoes, to truly understand and share their feelings, perspectives, and experiences. It goes beyond mere sympathy, as empathy enables us to connect with others on a deeper level and respond with genuine care and concern. When we practise empathy, we create a safe space for people to express themselves, fostering trust and emotional bonds.

Empathy also plays a crucial role in building stronger relationships. Whether it's with family, friends, colleagues, or strangers, our ability to empathise allows us to be more understanding, patient, and supportive. When we genuinely listen to others and validate their emotions, we enhance our communication and foster a sense of belonging.

Cultivating Empathy

1. Active Listening: Engage in active listening during conversations, giving your full attention to the speaker. Put aside distractions and truly focus on understanding their message.

2. Validate Emotions: Acknowledge and validate the emotions of others, even if you may not fully relate to their experiences. Let them know their feelings are important and understood.

3. Perspective-Taking: Put yourself in the other person's situation, considering their background, beliefs, and values. This helps to broaden your understanding and promote empathy.

4. Practise Empathic Responses: Respond to others with empathy and kindness. Use phrases like "I understand how you must be feeling" or "That sounds challenging, and I'm here to support you."

The Impact of Compassion

Compassion is a natural extension of empathy, as it involves taking action to alleviate the suffering of others. It involves recognizing their pain, feeling moved by it, and then actively responding with kindness and assistance. Compassion is a powerful force that not only benefits those we help but also enhances our own well-being.

When we practise compassion, we experience a sense of fulfilment and purpose. Engaging in acts of kindness releases feel-good hormones like oxytocin and endorphins, creating a positive feedback loop that reinforces our desire to continue helping others. As we contribute to the

well-being of others, we strengthen our
sense of interconnectedness and experience
a deeper sense of meaning in life.

Cultivating Compassion

1. Be of Service: Look for opportunities to be
of service to others. Offer your time, skills,
or resources to help those in need.

2. Random Acts of Kindness: Perform small
acts of kindness without expecting anything
in return. Simple gestures like holding the
door open, offering a compliment, or
lending a helping hand can brighten
someone's day.

3. Volunteer: Engage in volunteer work for a
cause that resonates with you. Giving back
to the community can be incredibly
rewarding and allows you to connect with
like-minded individuals.

4. Practice Self-Compassion: Extend compassion to yourself as well. Treat yourself with kindness and understanding, as this enables you to offer genuine compassion to others.

The Ripple Effect of Spreading Joy

When we practise empathy and compassion, we create a ripple effect of positivity that extends beyond the immediate recipients of our actions. Our kindness inspires others to do the same, creating a chain reaction of goodness in the world. One small act of compassion can lead to numerous acts of kindness, touching the lives of countless individuals.

Additionally, when we spread joy and positivity to others, we enhance our sense of interconnectedness and belonging. We become part of a larger community driven by empathy, compassion, and a shared desire to make the world a better place.

By impacting others positively through empathy and compassion, we contribute to a collective well-being that elevates everyone involved. As we continue on our journey of leading a good life, let us remember the immense power we hold to create meaningful and lasting change in the lives of others through these transformative qualities. By embracing empathy and compassion, we not only enrich the lives of others but also enrich our own lives in the process.

The Ripple Effect of Spreading Joy Within Communities

When individuals embrace happiness and make a conscious effort to spread positivity, it creates a ripple effect that extends far beyond their immediate surroundings. The interconnectedness of communities means that a single act of kindness can trigger a chain reaction, touching the lives of numerous individuals. Let's delve into how the ripple effect of spreading joy can transform communities for the better.

1. Building Stronger Bonds

When individuals within a community actively engage in spreading joy and kindness, it fosters a sense of camaraderie and strengthens social bonds. Acts of kindness can range from simple gestures, like helping a neighbour with their groceries, to more organised community initiatives, such as volunteering for local charities. Each act of kindness establishes a connection between the giver and the receiver, laying the foundation for a more compassionate and supportive community.

These bonds act as a safety net during difficult times, as individuals are more likely to lend a helping hand to those they feel connected to. As more community members participate in spreading joy, the bonds grow stronger, creating an environment where people look out for one another, fostering a sense of belonging and unity.

2. Inspiring Positive Change

The ripple effect of spreading joy within communities goes beyond immediate interactions. Acts of kindness can inspire others to follow suit, creating a domino effect of positive change. When people witness the impact of small acts of kindness, they are motivated to emulate them, perpetuating the cycle of spreading joy. This collective effort can lead to significant positive transformations in the community.

For instance, a single community cleanup event organised by a few passionate individuals can inspire others to join in. As more people participate, the community becomes cleaner and more beautiful, instilling a sense of pride and environmental responsibility. Through the collective efforts of community members, positive change becomes a shared goal, leading to an empowered and proactive community.

3. Enhancing Emotional Well-being

As the ripple effect of spreading joy unfolds, it significantly impacts the emotional well-being of community members. Research has shown that acts of kindness trigger the release of endorphins, often referred to as the "feel-good" hormones, in both the giver and the receiver. These neurochemicals promote feelings of happiness, reduce stress, and contribute to an overall sense of well-being.

When more individuals within a community engage in acts of kindness, the collective emotional state improves. People experience increased levels of happiness, empathy, and

emotional connection, which in turn fosters
a positive atmosphere in the community.
Reduced stress and anxiety levels can lead
to improved mental health, resulting in a
community that is more resilient and better
equipped to handle challenges.

4. Strengthening Community Support
Systems

The ripple effect of spreading joy within
communities can also strengthen existing
support systems or inspire the creation of
new ones. Acts of kindness often uncover
unmet needs within the community,
prompting individuals to collaborate and
find solutions together. This could lead to
the formation of support groups,
mentorship programs, or initiatives that
address specific challenges faced by
community members.

By supporting one another, communities
become more self-sufficient and better

equipped to address issues collectively. The support systems fostered through spreading joy can offer assistance to those in need, ensuring that no one feels isolated or neglected in times of difficulty.

Conclusion

Reflecting on the Journey to Living a Good Life

This book delved into the depths of human emotions, relationships, personal growth, and the pursuit of happiness. Our expedition began by acknowledging the universal yearning for happiness. From ancient philosophers to modern researchers, the pursuit of happiness has been an ever-present quest in human history. Happiness is not merely a fleeting moment of pleasure but rather a profound sense of joy that comes from within.

In this journey, exploring the significance of cultivating a positive mindset, has a profound impact on our emotions and actions, shaping the course of our lives. By recognizing and overcoming negative thought patterns, have a way for a brighter and more optimistic outlook. Through the practice of gratitude and appreciation, we can find joy even in the simplest of moments, enriching our daily experiences.

One of the most profound revelations on our expedition has been the power of meaningful relationships. It has a way to discover that our connections with others play a vital role in our overall happiness. Nurturing authentic friendships and strengthening family bonds have proven to be sources of profound joy. Having explored the importance of effective communication and emotional intelligence in sustaining healthy relationships, enriching our interactions with loved ones.

By identifying our core values and aligning our choices with them, it has unlocked the gateway to fulfilment. Having learned that pursuing goals that align with our passions can lead to a profound sense of purpose and satisfaction in life.

Mindfulness and self-compassion have been guiding lights on our expedition. The practice of mindfulness has allowed us to be present in the moment, savouring the beauty of life's journey. Additionally, by extending kindness and compassion to ourselves, we've freed ourselves from the chains of self-criticism and learned to embrace our imperfections with love and acceptance.

In our quest for a good life, we've learned the art of balance - balancing work, life, and leisure. Achieving work-life balance has been an essential aspect of our journey, as we've discovered that it fosters overall well-being and enhances our ability to enjoy leisure and hobbies. By incorporating moments of relaxation and downtime, we've cultivated a more harmonious and fulfilling existence.

Along our path, we've encountered challenges and adversity, but we've emerged stronger through resilience. Coping with life's difficulties has taught us valuable lessons in growth and adaptability.

Emphasising the Value of Embracing Joy Within

Throughout this book, having delved into various aspects of leading a fulfilling life, from fostering positive relationships to finding purpose, practising mindfulness, and navigating challenges with resilience. Now, let's focus on the pivotal lesson that lies at the heart of our exploration: the transformative power of embracing joy from within.

In a world that often bombards us with external pressures and expectations, it's all too easy to seek happiness in external achievements, possessions, or validations. However, the true essence of lasting happiness lies in discovering and nurturing the joy that resides within each one of us. Embracing joy from within isn't merely a fleeting moment of contentment; it's a fundamental shift in perspective that can shape the entirety of our lives.

Placing our focus on external factors to bring us happiness, we inadvertently relinquish control over our emotional well-being. It becomes dependent on circumstances, people, or events to dictate our levels of happiness, leading to a rollercoaster of emotions that can be exhausting and unpredictable. On the other hand, learning to cultivate joy from within, reclaiming the reins of our emotional state, fostering a sense of empowerment and agency over our lives.

Think of your internal joy as a wellspring of positive energy that you can tap into whenever life's challenges arise. It's an anchor that keeps you steady amidst the storms, a source of resilience that helps you bounce back from setbacks, and a guiding light that leads you toward a life of purpose and fulfilment. Embracing joy within doesn't mean ignoring external realities; rather, it's about cultivating an inner sanctuary of positivity that strengthens you to face those realities with grace and determination.

One of the remarkable aspects of embracing joy within is its ripple effect on the world around us. When we radiate positivity, kindness, and contentment from within, we naturally inspire those we interact with. Our relationships, whether with family, friends, colleagues, or even strangers, are enriched by our presence. People are drawn to those who exude authenticity and positivity, creating a circle of influence that can extend far beyond our immediate connections.

Furthermore, embracing joy from within contributes to our overall well-being. Scientific research consistently highlights the benefits of a positive mindset on physical health, mental resilience, and longevity. By prioritising our inner happiness, we actively invest in our own health and longevity, thereby increasing our capacity to enjoy life's precious moments to the fullest.

In the quest for a good life, remember that embracing joy from within is not a one-time achievement but an ongoing journey. It requires mindfulness, self-awareness, and continuous effort to cultivate positive habits and perspectives. Just as we tend to a garden to nurture its growth, we must tend to our inner landscape to allow the seeds of joy to flourish and blossom.

Encouraging Readers to Take Actionable Steps Toward Fulfilment

In conclusion to exploring the secrets to living a good life and embracing the joy within, it's important to recognize that knowledge alone isn't enough to transform our lives. To truly reap the benefits of the insights shared throughout this book, taking intentional and actionable steps that align with our newfound understanding. In this final section, the practical aspects of applying these principles to your life, empower you to embark on a fulfilling journey of self-discovery, growth, and happiness.

1.Setting Clear Intentions

Taking action begins with setting clear intentions for the kind of life you want to lead. Visualise your ideal future – what does it look like? How do you feel? What activities bring you joy? By crystallising your aspirations, you create a roadmap that guides your choices and actions. Remember, your intentions are the compass that will steer you toward a life rich with meaning and fulfilment.

2. Crafting Your Action Plan

Turning intentions into reality requires a well-thought-out action plan. Break down your larger goals into smaller, manageable steps. This approach not only makes your goals less daunting but also allows you to celebrate small victories along the way. For instance, if you're aiming to incorporate more physical activity into your routine, start with daily walks and gradually increase the intensity. Your action plan should be flexible, adapting to the changing circumstances of life while keeping your ultimate vision in mind.

3. Cultivating Consistent Habits

Consistency is the cornerstone of progress. Habits shape our lives, and consciously cultivating positive habits can lead to remarkable transformations. Choose habits that align with the principles discussed in this book, whether it's practising gratitude each morning, setting aside time for mindfulness, or engaging in acts of kindness. Consistency reinforces positive behaviours, making them a natural part of your daily routine.

4.Embracing Accountability and Support

Accountability and support play significant roles in our journey toward fulfilment. Share your goals and intentions with a trusted friend, family member, or mentor who can provide encouragement and gentle reminders. Additionally, consider joining communities or groups that share your interests and values. Surrounding yourself with like-minded individuals can foster a sense of belonging and provide an avenue for shared growth.

5.Celebrating Progress and Learning from Setbacks

Every step forward, no matter how small, is a reason to celebrate. Acknowledge your progress and pat yourself on the back for the efforts you've invested. Equally important, embrace setbacks as opportunities for growth. Challenges and failures are inevitable, but they provide valuable insights that can propel you further on your journey. Rather than viewing setbacks as roadblocks, see them as detours that ultimately lead you toward greater wisdom and resilience.

6.Continuing the Journey

As you embark on this journey of self-discovery and personal growth, remember that it's a continuous process. The pursuit of a fulfilling life is not a destination but a lifelong adventure. Embrace the idea that growth is ongoing, and your understanding of what it means to lead a good life will evolve over time. Stay open to new experiences, new perspectives,

and new insights that will enrich your
journey.

7.Your Story Matters

Finally, understand that your story matters.
Your experiences, your challenges, and your
triumphs contribute to the tapestry of your
life. Your unique journey is an inspiration to
others, and by sharing your story, you create
a ripple effect that extends beyond yourself.
As you take actionable steps toward
fulfilment, know that your efforts have the
potential to positively impact not only your
life but the lives of those around you.

In closing, I want to express my gratitude
for joining me on this exploration of
embracing the joy within and uncovering
the secrets for living a good life. The insights
you've gained and the actionable steps you'll
take are the keys to unlocking a life of
purpose, meaning, and happiness. May your

journey be filled with discovery, growth, and an abundance of joy.

I hope you find this section detailed and comprehensive, encouraging readers to take actionable steps toward fulfilment. Feel free to make any adjustments or let me know if there's anything else you'd like to include!